# Musical Form

## A N D

# Musical Performance

# Musical Form

## AND

# Musical Performance

❖❖❖❖❖❖❖❖❖❖❖❖❖❖❖❖❖

## EDWARD T. CONE

PROFESSOR EMERITUS OF MUSIC
PRINCETON UNIVERSITY

W · W · NORTON & COMPANY

New York · London

W. W. Norton & Company, Inc., 500 Fifth Avenue, New York, N.Y. 10110
W. W. Norton & Company Ltd., 10 Coptic Street, London, WC1A 1PU

ISBN 0-393-09767-6

PRINTED IN THE UNITED STATES OF AMERICA

1 2 3 4 5 6 7 8 9 0

# *Contents*

# Preface

The three essays on musical form and performance (to which the fourth has been added as an optional postlude) are revised and expanded versions of lectures given at the Conservatory of Music of Oberlin College during January 1967, as a part of its centennial celebration. I am indebted to the Theory Department of the Conservatory not only for inducing me, by its invitation, to try to put my thoughts into some kind of order, but also for providing me with a perceptive and stimulating audience.

My thanks are due also to the members of a seminar on analysis and performance that I conducted at Princeton University during the Fall term of 1966. They were forcibly exposed to the substance of these lectures in a crude and preliminary version, and their comments and criticisms helped me to arrive at a clearer formulation.

Finally, as the "onlie begetter" of much of the controlling thought of these pages I must acknowledge my teacher and friend Roger Sessions, although, to be sure, I must take full responsibility for my own possibly idiosyncratic interpretation and development of his suggestions. My ideas on phrase-rhythm—to take a single example—stem in great measure from a remark he once made in conversation (which he may have long forgotten!), while at the same time they owe much to his discussion in *The Musical Experience of Composer, Performer, Listener*.[1]

In recognition of an influence that, for me as for many

[1] Princeton, N.J.: Princeton University Press, 1950. See especially pp. 11-15

others, has proved seminal, I should like to dedicate this little volume to him as an inadequate installment on a debt that can never be paid in full.

EDWARD T. CONE

*Princeton, N. J.*
*June, 1967.*

# Musical Form

## AND

# Musical Performance

# I

⟨✦⟨✦⟨✦⟨✦⟨✦⟨✦

# THE PICTURE

# AND THE FRAME

## *The Nature*

## *of Musical Form*

---

It has been said that some of the most important scientific discoveries have resulted from taking seriously questions that are usually assumed to be trivial. Thus, the complete answer to "Why does it get dark at night?" leads to the theory of the expanding universe. The questions I shall propound, although sufficiently trivial, will, I fear, lead to no such momentous conclusions. I hope only that, if taken seriously, they will throw some light on a problem that is manifestly by no means trivial: how to achieve valid and effective musical performance.

The first and last word on this subject was spoken by the King of Hearts. Although he was telling the White Rabbit specifically how to read verse, his advice speaks clearly to all performing artists: "Begin at the beginning, . . . and go on till you come to the end: then stop." And this brings me to my first set of foolish questions: Where is the beginning of a piece of music? Where is the end?

Now, the moment one tries to take these questions seriously, one realizes that they can be applied only to a certain type of music, namely, music with a beginning and an end —or, since, the world being what it is, everything has a beginning and an end, music of which these are essential parts. To a great deal of music, beginnings and ends (let us call them extremes) not only are not essential, but at best are simply necessary interruptions. When modern social dancing became non-formal (in the sense of ceasing to require conformity to rules of deportment and prescribed orders of steps), pauses between dances became non-functional. The ideal music for the ballroom of today would be continuous, so that the dancers could begin and end whenever they liked. As it is, the pauses are only those enforced by the exhaustion of the band or the changing of a record. Similarly, military marches, even though they may need beginnings, should have no endings: they have to stop whenever the order is given. (Hence the ideal march would theoretically be one that could stop at any point and still make musical sense—surely a challenge to the ingenuity of a composer.) Background music, whether at the cocktail hour or during the intermission of a play, should be essentially continuous and nondescript—like wallpaper, as Satie tried to demonstrate with his indefinitely repeatable *Vexations*.

All this music is, of course, functional: it is not really meant to be listened to, only to be heard. But there are also kinds of functional music whose effectiveness depends in part on the existence of a listening audience. Music for a religious service, whether it tries to be purely liturgical, historically evocative, or directly expressive, depends for its effect on the attentiveness of the congregation. And even though the organ prelude has begun before most of us arrive, just as the postlude goes on after we leave, what we do hear of the one should act as a transition between our worldly activities and the service to come, while the other should send us away with some bit of Heaven still lying about us. This they can do only if we let them—by listening to them. (Because they are incompletely heard, Bach fugues are wasted on these occasions. One might perhaps compose a prelude without a beginning, and a postlude without an ending, just for this use—or possibly a single piece, designed to have its second half played first and its first half last.)

In spite of these borderline cases, the distinction between music to be listened to and music to be merely heard is an important one. It should be remembered every time we are tempted to turn on the local "good music" station as a background for reading or conversation. It should also be recalled by those who sit silently and solemnly through performances of divertimenti obviously written to be used as dinner-music.

When I use the term *art* to distinguish music meant to be listened to, I intend no invidious comparison; I am only trying to define the music we shall henceforth be dealing with. Furthermore, if a piece is to qualify as a *work of art*, that is to say, as a real *composition*, not only must it have extremes, but these must be generated by the music itself—and not solely by the exigencies of an external function. Finally, in order for a composition—i.e. a piece composed as a work of art—to behave as one, its extremes must be respected in performance.

A proper musical performance must thus be a dramatic, even a theatrical event, presenting as it does an action with a beginning, a middle, and an end—hence an action of a certain completeness within itself. This dramatic quality must be present whether the performance is entirely private, as when one reads music silently or plays it over to oneself, or whether there is a public, which can of course vary in size from one or two to a whole concert-audience. A play remains a play, after all, whether we read it to ourselves, act it out privately, or put it on the stage.

Now we are back to our original trivial question, which we can expand and clarify a bit: If the performance of a composition must respect its extremes, exactly how are these to be defined? Does a composition necessarily begin with the first note and end with the last one? Are the periods of time before and after a composition ever parts of it?

We can point up the problem by contrasting music with almost any kind of literature or drama. The formal extremes of a play are indicated by the rise and fall of the curtain; but the exposed action is always only an episode in the flow of historic or mythic time. The causes of Hamlet's tragedy occurred long before the opening scene, and its consequences continue indefinitely after the last act. No matter how complete in scope a novel may attempt to be, one can always ask, "What happened before? What happens afterward?" In fact, in our entire Western tradition, I can think offhand of only two literary works that presuppose no prior time (Genesis and The Gospel According to St. John), and none (not even The Revelation or the *Paradiso*) that achieves real finality.

Turning to painting, we find that the edge of the picture demarcates that portion of a subject chosen for representation, but every depicted scene necessarily extends indefinitely outside its delimiting boundaries. Even in the case of abstractions, one can usually imagine the pattern as continuing beyond the picture-area. The edge is essential if a picture is to be viewed as a work of art, as one can discover by looking at pictures without edges, like Pozzo's ceiling for S. Ignazio in Rome. There is great art in the ceiling, but it is not a work of art, nor was it intended as such: it is a part of another work of art, namely, the church itself.

The frame of a picture is the intensification of the edge. It works in two directions. It marks the limits not only of the picture, but also of the real world around the picture

—of the wall on which the picture hangs. In the same way theatrical conventions—the lowering of the lights, the curtain—act as frames; and the typographical layout of a book, a story, or a poem, implies a frame. In every case its function is twofold. First, it separates the subject chosen for treatment from its own imagined surroundings—what I call the *internal environment*: second, it protects the work from the encroachment of its *external environment*, that is, of the real time and space in which the perceiver lives. The frame announces: Here the real world leaves off and the work of art begins; here the work of art ends and the real world takes up again.

We can now recognize an important way in which music differs from these other arts: it has no internal environment. A composition cannot be thought of as a delimited segment of a longer line. It has no antecedents and no consequents. Whatever music may be about—and I do not wish to raise that issue—the "whatever" begins only when the music begins, and ends when the music ends. This may be why musical finality is so complete, and why many people find operas more emotionally satisfying than plays.

One might try to argue that music—at least some music—does have a kind of internal environment in the form of its abstract system—be it tonal, atonal, or twelve-tonal—which in a sense existed before and continues after the concrete composition. But this is merely like saying that the grammar of a language, or indeed the language itself, pre-exists and survives statements in that language. If we accept this analogy, we see that we are confusing two different temporal dimensions. A grammar does not exist before, or during, or after any statement; it is essentially timeless. Like systems of mathematics or logic it is, so to speak, eternal. In the same way, a musical system may be thought of as *subsisting* independently of its embodiments, but not as *existing* in their time-continuum. (On the other hand, music that is intrinsically formless, in the sense of having no apparent musical reason for beginning and ending when and as it does, may sound like an arbitrarily framed segment of an indefinitely extending sound-continuum. This is indeed the effect of much "totally organized" serial music, and equally of much music composed by methods of pure chance.)

For most music then, internal environment is a meaningless concept. In spite of this fact, or perhaps because of it, music stands in great need of a frame to separate it from its external environment—to mark off musical time from the ordinary time before it and after it. Without such a frame, the chaotic, undifferentiated flow of ordinary time will encroach on each extreme of the composition. It will prevent us at the beginning from being aware of the measure of temporal control exerted by the music, and at the end from appreciating the full discharge of its energy. At this point you have undoubtedly guessed what the frame is. It is silence.

If we are members of an audience, silence should present to us a period of empty time in which *nothing* is happening. It should separate our individual and collective movements from the movement that is, for the time being, to control us all: the music. This is why the singer waits for the latecomers to be seated and for the coughing to stop. This is why the conductor poises his baton. This is why we do not want him to conduct an empty measure (although if he is leading amateurs he may have to): that would be something happening just before the music starts, and *nothing* should be happening then.

Similarly, at the end, we need silence to cover our return to ordinary time. That is why the sensitive listener waits before applauding—and why the superlative performance enjoins silence rather than applause. True, by this token either most audiences—and especially opera-audiences—are peculiarly insensitive, or most performances are something less than superlative. Of course one often does hear exciting interpretations that build up so much energy that the overflow is imparted to the audience, which has to respond by immediate clapping; but I wonder whether these performances are not, for that very reason, a bit meretricious. Leo Stein has suggested that music requiring bodily motion on the part of the listener for its complete enjoyment, like much popular dance music, is by that token artistically imperfect; [1] perhaps the same principle can be applied to performance.

The decision as to the nature of the time between the movements of a longer work is often difficult, for at least three possibilities must be considered. If the connections are clearly meant to be *attacca*, as in Beethoven's *Sonata quasi una fantasia*, Op. 27, No. 1, the time between movements is as much a part of the piece as internal pauses, such as those that so strikingly interrupt the first movement of Schumann's Fantasy, Op. 17. In another case one may decide that, although each movement is separate, performers and audience should have no "free" time between movements—that these moments represent frame, like the intermediate frames of a triptych. Or one may wish to give the performers a chance to time up, and the audience a chance to rest: now the members of the triptych have been separated and placed at intervals along the wall. This is the case with most classical concertos—which demand applause at the end of the first movement at least—and, for obvious reasons, with most symphonies by Bruckner and Mahler. The first two kinds of performance are somewhat overworked today, and often used against the clear intentions of the composer. The modish demand for silence between movements not only inhibits spontaneous demonstrations of enjoyment, but also often imposes such a strain on the listener that he cannot attend properly to the latter half of a long symphony.

The existence of *attacca* connections and the occurrence of general pauses within movements point to yet another interesting possibility. Perhaps some of the silence immedi-

[1] Leo Stein, *The ABC of Aesthetics,* New York: Horace Liveright, 1927, pp. 197-98.

ately before and after a composition is actually a part, not of the frame, but of the work itself. Now, it is hard to imagine how any performer, short of indulging in ludicrous silent conducting or other equally inappropriate actions, could indicate the beginning of a piece prior to the first attack. (This is one reason why Riemann's doctrine of a universal upbeat, implied where it is not explicit, is unacceptable.) On the other hand, a clearly defined metrical pattern often imposes itself on the final chord of a composition—especially when it is a very strong downbeat—in such a way as to force several beats or even several measures into the ensuing silence. Standard notational practice supports this differentiation. Composers as a rule open a score either with the first attack, or with the minimum number of rests essential for easy reading; but they often end with indications of extra time—by *fermatas* or even blank measures. But where this is not done, the implication of silent measures is still often inescapable. The score of Beethoven's Fifth Symphony begins with an eighth rest, but surely this is a device to prevent misreading of the triple upbeat that follows. No one can hear it as a silent downbeat. At the end of the movement, however, the four-measure pattern has been so firmly established that one is forced to add a silent measure after the last one notated—a measure that is as essentially a part of the composition as those actually written.

The principle that a composition begins at its first attack applies equally to those that start, like the Fifth Symphony, with a clear upbeat, and to those that start, like the Seventh, with a clear downbeat. In each case, there is a demarcation between the attack and the preceding silence. But the Ninth exemplifies a kind of beginning that was, so far as I know, new with Beethoven, but became increasingly popular during the nineteenth century: the almost imperceptible growth of sound from silence—in rhythmic terms, the gradual emergence of a huge upbeat. In such cases we feel, in retrospect, that the music may have been going on for some time, below the threshold of hearing, before it became loud enough for us to perceive it. If this is so, then one must grant retroactively to the preliminary silence a share in the actual composition. In the same way, works like *Das Lied von der Erde,* with its final direction of *gänzlich ersterbend,* should at the last fade imperceptibly into the time following, so that any decision as to when the music is really over must be arbitrary. Debussy, in *Brouillards,* goes one step further in this direction. Here the score, and therefore what we actually hear, comes to an end before the final resolution to the tonic. If we are to hear it at all, we must supply it in our own imaginations.

Another form of indistinct edge is found in what one might call an irruptive opening: one that breaks in so violently as to suggest that there should be *no* silence before it, no frame to separate the music from the outer world. The storm in *Otello,* for example, should, ideally, start while the audience is still applauding the entrance of the conductor: the music itself should enforce attention. Here, too, Beethoven may have been a forerunner, for I have heard a most effective performance of Op 111 that began in just this way.

The corresponding type of close is represented by some of Bruckner's symphonies. No matter how long he extends the final tonic, it never seems quite long enough, and the following silence always comes as a shock. The only solution, then, would seem to be for the applause to break in immediately. (Would the same solution apply to the end of *Wozzeck,* different though it is? I have never heard a convincing performance of the oscillating triplets, which do not end, but merely stop.)

One might compare music that overflows its frame with some of Piranesi's engravings, in which a depicted building pushes through the conventional frame without, however, destroying it. The contrast between art of clearly defined extremes and that with blurred edges reveals, of course, one distinction between classical and romantic forms—a distinction that manifests itself on many levels. *The Marriage of Figaro,* dealing with a circumscribed action restricted to a single day, uses delimited forms whose outlines, from the overture to the finale, are exactly perceptible. The action of the *Ring,* which covers an entire epoch, is accompanied by music as nearly continuous as possible. With the Prelude of *Das Rheingold,* a whole world rises from nothing, from the time before time; it returns to nothing with the end of *Götterdämmerung.*

In our own day all bars seem to be down, so that it is often impossible to distinguish works of art (whatever their medium) from either frame or surrounding world. In an art gallery today one is often unsure as to which objects are meant to be looked at and which to be treated as furniture. In the same way it is sometimes hard, in listening to what Varèse called "organized sound," to know which sounds are organized and which are fortuitous—i.e. which are elements of the composition and which are external noises. (At the world première of Varèse's *Déserts* in Paris, in the Fall of 1954, radio listeners could not distinguish between the music and the noise of the demonstration by unfriendly members of the audience.) Cage, of course, revels in such ambiguities. As is well-known, he once "wrote" and "performed" a composition that, according to the foregoing definition, consisted entirely of four minutes and thirty-three seconds of frame.

Some contemporary art-forms exaggerate a related tendency toward an overflow, not so much of the frame, as of the very dimensions of the medium. What I have in mind is illustrated in earlier periods by *trompe-l'oeil* details on a painting—the fly that one tries to brush off the Petrus Christus portrait in the New York Metropolitan Museum—or by the characters in a play who speak directly to the audience. This attempt to create an extra dimensionality by involving the real world of the spectator is of course especially successful in the theater—witness Genet's *Les Nègres,* not to speak of those events referred to as "happenings." Musical parallels might be found in performances of Berlioz's

Requiem that, by placing the brass choirs around the audience (in violation of the composer's original intention), include the listeners themselves in the performance, or in electronic compositions (e.g. the original version of Varèse's *Poème électronique*) that are designed to be projected from all sides of a hall. For absolute music, however, the parallel is not exact. In such cases the physical involvement of the audience cannot be said to add an extra dimension; all it does is to allow them a closer approach to the normal experience of the performer, who is almost always in the midst of the music. Active listening is, after all, a kind of vicarious performance, effected, as Sessions puts it, by "inwardly reproducing" the music [2]—which, I take it, is also what Hindemith means by "mental coconstruction." [3] To be included within the physical space devoted to sound-production may well prove very exciting to the listener, but rather through the intensification of his normal reactions than through the stimulation of novel ones. Thus, from the programmatic point of view, it may be true that the listener surrounded by Berlioz's *Tuba mirum* does indeed feel a special identification with the awakening dead of the Last Judgment; if this is the case, then the work as a whole moves into a new dimension—but a dramatic one. From the purely musical point of view the listener is only experiencing a sense of participation that he could (theoretically, at least) enjoy quite independently of the placing of the brasses—by playing in the orchestra or singing in the chorus! (The same distinction can, I think, be applied to electronic music. For the trained listener who can, in imagination, "perform" an electronic work in a completely abstract way, its spatial aspects will take their place as part of the "orchestration." For most of the audience, on the other hand, their effect will add an obscurely programmatic

[2] Roger Sessions, *The Musical Experience of Composer, Performer, Listener*, Princeton, N.J.: Princeton University Press, 1950, p. 97.
[3] Paul Hindemith, *A Composer's World*, Cambridge, Mass.: Harvard University Press, 1952, p. 17.

dimension, and their effectiveness will depend thereon.)

So far we have been considering the various relationships possible between the musical composition on the one hand and its environment on the other. Now we must begin to look within the composition itself, and here we encounter a different kind of frame. Just as silence can be forced to become part of the music it surrounds, so occasionally the extremes of a composition become separated from the body of the work in such a way that they act as what we might call internal frames. Familiar examples are to be found in the last of Beethoven's Bagatelles, Op. 126, and in Mendelssohn's *Song without Words* No. 9 (*Consolation*). In each of these the introduction is complete and self-contained, arriving at a full cadence; in each the same material returns, without change, to form the coda. They are thus a part, yet not wholly a part, of the composition. They set off the rest like the depicted window frames through which we sometimes see the subject of a Dutch portrait, or the abstract lines by which Marin encloses his seascapes. Another analogy is suggested by the device that the Germans, significantly enough, call the *Rahmenerzählung*—the story within a story.

Complete structures like the above are comparatively uncommon. Framing codas are especially rare, for what we call a coda is usually harmonically and rhythmically demanded by what precedes it and is an essential part of the form. "Peroration" would often be a more appropriate term. Frame-like introductions are more frequent. Sometimes they are quite elaborate, but expansion always carries with it the danger of excessive independence. The introduction to Tchaikovsky's First Piano Concerto, in spite of half-hearted attempts to lead into the Allegro, remains essentially an over-developed frame that fails to integrate itself with the rest of the movement. The framing introduction of *Also sprach Zarathustra*, although more intimately connected motivically with what follows, nevertheless arrives at a climax so big that the rest of the tone-poem almost sounds like an afterthought.

In contradistinction to these examples, most introductions, even when differentiated from what follows by both tempo and theme, prepare for and lead into the body of the work and should therefore not be performed as semi-independent frames. Such openings serve a variety of functions. Sometimes the introduction is at least partly practical, as when it enables a singer to secure his pitch. Sometimes it builds up dramatic tension to be released by the main movement. From the purely musical point of view, it can suggest the essential tonal, metrical, or dynamic space of the work as a whole. The first two measures of the *Eroica*, for example, establish all three: they reiterate the chord that will turn out to be the tonic; they punctuate the strong beats of the measures; and they indicate the power of the full orchestra in contrast to the relatively quiet theme to follow. They even adumbrate this theme, which begins, after all, as an arpeggiation of the introductory chord.

In every respect, then, the beginning of the *Eroica* is conceived as a completely integrated introduction, not as a mere frame. How can this distinction be realized in performance? Only by respecting the basic rhythmic character of these two measures: by recognizing that they constitute an upbeat. No matter that they are *forte* and the ensuing theme *piano*, that they are *tutti* and the theme, as it were, *concertino*—their basic role is vitiated unless they are somehow conducted and played to be heard as a double upbeat. Although the strings would hardly use up-bow, keeping such a possibility in mind would suggest the requisite lightness and springiness; the heavy accents we so often get almost drown out the theme and prevent a convincing start. Furthermore, an upbeat performance of these measures stresses their kinship both with the parallel measures of dominant harmony immediately preceding the recapitulation, and with the two balancing measures of tonic afterbeat at the very end.

These two measures thus offer us a clue to the basic im-

portance of the introduction, an explanation of its fre-
quency: an introduction is an expanded upbeat. Even
when, as in Beethoven's Seventh Symphony, it is long, begins with its own strong downbeat, and contains many sub-
divisions—a true introduction, as opposed to a frame, is an
expanded upbeat. A careful distinction between the two
types is necessary for intelligent performance. (One must
also be careful to distinguish a true introduction from one in
name only. The orchestral ritornello of a baroque concerto
or aria is often incorrectly called an introduction. In point
of fact it is usually the first statement of a principal theme.
The role of the opening tutti of a classical concerto is more
complex, but its expository character usually predominates.
This may explain why Beethoven at least once preceded it
by a true introduction.)

This concept of an expanded upbeat—a preparation for
the basic progression of the piece—is so pervasive that we
find it penetrating many compositions lacking an overt introduction. It is especially clear in compositions that begin
away from the tonic, such as Beethoven's Sonata, Op. 31,
No. 3. But even in Op. 53, which does begin squarely on
the tonic, the first theme pauses as if to *reculer pour mieux
sauter.* The beginning of Schubert's posthumous Sonata in
C minor, again on the tonic, exhibits no apparent pause,
but the opening leads directly to a submediant so greatly
expanded as to represent a written-out fermata; only after
it leads cadentially through the dominant back to the tonic
does the movement really get under way.

Of all the Beethoven symphonies, only the Eighth begins
with an unmistakeable downbeat and proceeds uninterrupt-
edly from the beginning. It is the exception that disproves
the rule, or rather that prevents the over-hasty gen-
eralization that all pieces begin with an actual or implied
introduction. Yet notice that even here it is the elided cadence of measure 12 that really sets things in motion. It is
one of those important points of simultaneous harmonic and
rhythmic arrival that I call a structural downbeat, for it is so

powerful that retrospectively it turns what precedes it into its own upbeat.

It is interesting to see how later nineteenth-century composers, by postponing further and further the appearance of the tonic, expand the initial upbeat to the point that it can hardly be called either preparatory or introductory. The search for the structural downbeat has itself become the basic progression. Brahms's little Intermezzo in B flat, Op. 76, No. 4, finds a downbeat only at the deceptive cadence that marks the end of its first section. An even more extraordinary accomplishment is the opening of the first movement of Schumann's Fantasy, in which the tonic downbeat arrives only at the end of the huge exposition, with the appearance of the middle section, "Im Legenden-Ton," that takes the place of the development. But compositions such as these, in pushing the arrival of a structural downbeat so far from the beginning, only exaggerate the natural periodicity by which music normally proceeds: tension followed by relaxation. To this extent, at least, Riemann's insistence on the universality of the upbeat was on the right track.

At this point we have obviously entered a new phase of our investigations; what occupies us is no longer "where does a composition begin (or end)?"—but "how?" In a word, we are dealing with the essentials of form. And musical form, as I conceive it, is basically rhythmic. It is not, as conventional analysis would have it, thematic, nor, *pace* Schenker, harmonic. Both of these aspects are important, but rhythm is basic. That is why Ravel could have said, as the story goes, that he had finished his composition—"all but the themes."

It would be an oversimplification to state, as I have been on the verge of doing, that every tonal composition represents a variation on a single rhythmic form, viz., an extended upbeat followed by its downbeat. Yet the oversimplification would not be a gross one. Just as, in a normal musical period, the antecedent phrase stands in some

sense as an upbeat to the consequent, so in larger forms
one entire section can stand as an upbeat to the next. And
if, as I believe, there is a sense in which a phrase can be
heard as an upbeat to its own cadence, larger and larger
sections can also be so apprehended. A completely unified
composition could then constitute a single huge rhythmic
impulse, completed at the final cadence. This does not necessarily mean, of course, the final chord. The ultimate resolution often requires a feminine ending—sometimes quite
extended—as a way of discharging its momentum. Such
endings are true codas, as opposed to perorations on the
one hand and frames on the other. (A very clear example is
the passage over the concluding tonic pedal in Bach's
Fugue in C minor, *Well-Tempered Clavier*, Book I. Another is to be found in the last four measures of Chopin's
Prelude in B minor. In performance, true codas like these
usually represent a diminuendo.)

    If such notions are to be useful, they need refinement;
and the place to start is the single phrase, which, if I am
right, is a microcosm of the composition. The classical
phrase has often been analyzed as an alternation of strong
and weak measures, on an analogy with strong and weak
beats within a measure. In other words, the larger rhythmic structure is treated simply as metric structure on a
higher level. Now, I do not deny that such alternation often
occurs, especially in the case of short, fast measures; but I
insist that on some level this metric principle of parallel
balance must give way to a more organic rhythmic principle that supports the melodic and harmonic shape of the
phrase and justifies its acceptance as a formal unit. Such a
principle must be based on the highly abstract concept of
musical energy, so it may be useful to approach it through
a concrete analogy. If I throw a ball and you catch it, the
completed action must consist of three parts: the throw,
the transit, and the catch. There are, so to speak, two fixed
points: the initiation of the energy and the goal toward
which it is directed; the time and distance between them

are spanned by the moving ball. In the same way, the typical musical phrase consists of an initial downbeat (⌐), a period of motion (◡), and a point of arrival marked by a cadential downbeat (◝). Unlike the undifferentiated transit of the ball, the musical passage is marked by stronger and weaker points (− ◡), but all of these are structurally light in comparison with the accented initial and terminal points. My analysis thus differs from that of Cooper and Meyer,[4] in its attempt to distinguish three types of "strong" points: the initial, the terminal, and the medial. An initial downbeat is marked by the kind of accent that implies a following *diminuendo;* a cadential downbeat suggests rather the goal of a *crescendo.* Medial strong points vary with the context. If the cadence, as the goal of the motion, is felt as even stronger than the initial downbeat, then the phrase does indeed become in a sense an expanded upbeat followed by a downbeat, the initial downbeat thereby accepting a reduced role as "the downbeat of the upbeat." But, as we shall see, because of the greater demands of the composition as a whole, not every phrase should be so considered.

If we wish to follow the ball-playing analogy a little further, we can imagine the thrower's wind-up as a preliminary anacrusis (ʌ), and the catcher's rebound as a feminine ending (v). (Or perhaps in this case he has dropped the ball!) I do not intend these comparisons seriously, of course, but they do point up the differences in character between these two rhythmic elements, as well as between these two on the one hand and medial weak beats or measures (◡) on the other. Such details do not alter but merely elaborate the standard form of the phrase, which could be depicted thus: (ʌ) ⌐ ◡ ◝ (v). To go a little further, one might think of an elision (◡⌐) as a return

---

[4] Grosvenor W. Cooper and Leonard B. Meyer, *The Rhythmic Structure of Music,* Chicago: University of Chicago Press, 1960. This book develops a method previously presented by Meyer in *Emotion and Meaning in Music,* Chicago: University of Chicago Press, 1956.

in tennis, which converts a catch into a fresh throw. The elision, as a matter of fact, demonstrates one advantage of this analysis. Since both cadential and initial measures are strong, the elision can be heard as a natural unification of the two.

At this point an example is in order. Let us look at the opening of Mozart's Piano Sonata in A major (K. 331), which consists of two four-measure phrases. If we try the conventional alternation of strong and weak measures we meet with little success. An initial light measure contradicts the firm opening tonic. An initial strong measure weakens the cadences excessively. They are, to begin with, structurally feminine; i.e. the final dominant or tonic enters on a relatively weak beat. To make the entire cadential mea-

sure weak in each case would create doubly feminine cadences—nay, in the first phrase, because of its postponed resolution, a triply feminine one! The resulting emphasis on the beginning of the third measure of each phrase would be hard to make convincing in performance, for it is only after this point that the consequent begins to differ from the antecedent. Besides, the sforzando in the penultimate measure throws emphasis forward in such a way as to suggest that the concluding measure, even though piano, is cadentially strong.

Let us now see what motivic and melodic harmonic analysis may reveal. The first phrase consists of two individual sequential measures followed by a two-measure unit:

$$\overbrace{\underset{a}{1}}\ \overbrace{\underset{a}{1}}\ \overbrace{\underset{b}{2}}$$

But the b itself can again be subdivided in the same way: two half-measure units (which can be heard as compressions of the original motif) plus a full measure. Both these relationships can be embodied in the following scheme, which embeds the one in the other. The cadential half of the phrase is itself a small rhythmic unit, whose cadential half in turn is the last bar.

The above pattern is confirmed by the over-all melodic-harmonic shape of the phrase, which, in spite of the line descending from the high E, I take to be primarily a movement away from and back to the original position of the tonic chord, followed by the (feminine) cadence.

The second phrase is a little different. Its third measure uncovers a relationship that was hidden the first time: the fact that the rise from A to C♯ can be heard as a third member of the original sequence. (At the same time, another sequence, a concealed one of two members—E–D–C♯ and D–C♯–B in the top voice—comes more clearly to the fore. This is the one that Schenker considered as governing the

entire period.[5]) As a result of the rhythmic shift, the step-
wise descent of the bass from tonic to dominant is more
clearly perceptible, for the E now comes on the strong half
of the last measure. This, together with the previously mentioned sforzando, points toward the pattern:

$$m.\left|\overset{5}{\phantom{x}}\smile\right|\overset{6}{\phantom{x}}\smile\left|\overset{7}{\phantom{x}}\smile\right|\overset{8}{\phantom{x}}\searrow v\,\bigg|$$

The final cadence, even though feminine, thus receives
more weight than the half-cadence. The entire period,
then, can be understood as an upbeat antecedent followed

by a downbeat consequent: ⌣ — . (For patterns at this level I find the neutral symbols ⌣ and — adequate, and, because of their familiarity, preferable.)

It is probably unnecessary to insist here that there is no necessary correlation between strong measures and dynamic accents, any more than a sforzando like the one in m. 7 indicates a metrically strong beat. Dynamic variation is only one of the means a good performer will use to indicate—as obviously or as delicately as the context demands —the shape of the phrase. Subtle temporal adjustments (e.g. agogic accent and rubato) are equally at his disposal. Of course, the more explicitly the rhythmic form has been written into the music, the less the performance is required to add. The entrance of the recapitulation in the first movement of the *Eroica* will always sound like a huge structural downbeat, regardless of performance!

If we look a little further into the Mozart example, we find that the first period is followed by a contrasting section, after which the original material, shortened and otherwise modified, returns to complete a typical ABA. From the point of view of the whole, the opening period can be considered as an expanded initial downbeat and the return as a cadential downbeat. Within the return, too, one could even hear the first four piano measures as an upbeat to the final two forte measures. The theme as a whole, then, exhibits in a complex way the basic form ⌣ ⌣ ⌣ . 

mm. 1 - 4 | 5 - 8 :‖: 9 - 12 | 13 - 16 | 17 - 18 :‖

At this point let us recall our basic problem, which was how to achieve valid and effective performance. Here we have found at least one answer: by discovering and making clear the rhythmic life of a composition. If I am right in locating musical form in rhythmic structure, it is the fundamental answer.

꙳꙳꙳꙳꙳꙳꙳

# II

# INSIDE THE PICTURE

## *Problems of*
## *Performance*

---

Sooner or later every discussion of the problems of musical performance seems to raise the question of the ideal interpretation: is there such a thing? Does one perfect performance of a composition subsist as the ideal toward which every actual one should aspire? Is this true of every composition? Is it true of any?

Most people would probably agree that, even if a perfect interpretation is conceivable, it is hardly possible of achievement, and that every actual performance must be at best an approximation of it. Still, many of us are vaguely comforted by the notion of one interpretation that, in some Platonic realm, constitutes *the* music as precisely as a picture is a picture, a statue is a statue, and a building is a building. According to this view, the space arts are fortunate, since they are fixed and unchanging; the time arts

(which would include drama and all other forms of literature as well as music) are subject to readings, performances, and interpretations, all of which distort the true
essence of the work of art. Nevertheless, this essence remains there, somewhere, to be discovered and, so far as
possible, exposed.

Unfortunately, this view is false even to the facts about
the space arts. For we read pictures, statues, and buildings,
just as surely as we read poems. We cannot view them simultaneously; we must choose our own paths through them
and work out for ourselves, as we go along, their various
inner relationships and meanings. As Leo Stein says, "[the
visual elements of a picture] indicate far more possible re-
lations amongst each other than any one can possibly get
hold of at any instant." [1] Just as we can call every reading
of a poem—even a silent one—a performance, so we might
say that really to look at a picture or to view a statue from
all sides or to walk through a building, is to perform the
picture or statue or building. Actually, the contemplation of
a work of spatial art almost always involves not one but
several performances—or at least several partial performances. We look from side to side, up and down, diagonally
and spirally, taking our time and clarifying for our own satisfaction first one and then another connection. It would be
a simple work, indeed, all of whose relationships became
clear at a glance—so simple, in fact, as hardly to constitute
a work of art at all.

This silent viewing of a spatial work, then, is a kind of
multiple performance—and it is not unlike the silent reading of a poem, or of a piece of music. Here, too, we can
choose our own pace, speed up or slow down as we like,
look back or ahead, pause, repeat—again, a multiple performance, or a multiplicity of partial performances. But
when we read a poem aloud, or actually play a piece of
music, we must choose a single complete performance. The
more complex the poem or the composition, the more re-

[1] *Op. cit.*, p. 86.

lationships its performance must be prepared to explain—
and the less likelihood that a single performance can ever
do the job. The composition must proceed inexorably in
time; we cannot go back to explain; we must therefore decide what is important and make that as clear as possible,
even at the expense of other aspects of the work. After all,
there will be other performances! Every valid interpretation thus represents, not an approximation of some ideal,
but a choice: which of the relationships implicit in this
piece are to be emphasized, to be made explicit?

A familiar example may make this point clearer. In the
opening of his C minor Prelude, Chopin has indicated that
each of the first two measures is to be phrased as a unit, but
that the next two measures are to be grouped together.

Now, the first two measures form a clear sequence, from

which the following two measures vary slightly. But there is a way of playing the bass of mm. 3 and 4, clearly suggested by its almost palindromic form, that produces a third member of the same sequence, only in augmentation.

So far so good; but suppose that, looking a little further, we find another relation—one equally important, but incompatible in the same performance with the previous one? Harmonically, one can hear m. 3 as revolving around F, and m. 4 around G. In that case, the entire progression of mm. 1–5 can be heard as an expansion of the I–IV–V–I of the opening measure. (Incidentally, the arrival of the tonic in m. 5, piano after the preceding fortissimo, is a beautiful example of a structural downbeat announced by a negative dynamic correlation.)

Which of the two relationships is to be brought out? Both are certainly present, and both are important—if only because both seem to resolve the problem of the notoriously disputed E♭ E♮ of m. 3 in favor of E♮, each analysis thus corroborating the other. Whatever decision one makes, one gains something, but one also loses something.

Fortunately such choices need not be permanent. They ought not to be. Even the performance that seems a revelation may become boring through repetition. This is why recorded performances inevitably lose their excitement and sometimes eventually become unbearable. (Reginald Kell's phrasing, which seemed so sensitive when one first bought his record of the Mozart Clarinet Concerto, may have come to sound impossibly mannered!) Besides, as time passes we look at compositions in new ways. What is now obvious may be forgotten and need to be pointed out again; what is now unclear may become tomorrow's cliché. Interpretation must take such changes into account and change with them.

Composers of electronic music imply by virtue of their activity—and sometimes explicitly state—that a single perfect performance can actually be realized—and by the composer himself. Now, composers may on occasion prove to be the best performers of their own music, but it is by no means logically necessary that they always must be. (I am sure that we have all experienced counter-examples.) Because of their intimate association with their own works, composers often fail to appreciate the way these will sound to those less familiar with them; hence they are by no means ideal judges of performances of these works— whether by others or by themselves. Their own performances, for example, may understate points that need to be emphasized for the sake of the listener, while devoting great care to subtleties that may not really be heard. Such a performance may teach a lot to one who already knows the composition well; but in the case of electronic music it is the only performance of a work for which there is often not even a readable score.

It might be argued that electronic music differs from conventional music in kind, much as cinema differs from theater. In these new media, one might say, the performance *is* the work of art. It is certainly true that, if a new version of a cinema classic were made today, using the original shooting script, it would be judged, not as a new performance, but as an entirely new movie. Similarly, on this view, any change in the "performance" of an electronic work would constitute a compositional change, performance and composition being in this case one. Such an argument may indeed clarify the nature of electronic music, but it does not prove the possibility of ideal performances. It could lead equally well to the conclusion that electronic compositions must always be imperfect.

At any rate, whether one decides that an electronic performance is, like a conventional performance, one possible realization of an independent musical entity, or that it is the unique embodiment of its own music—in either case one is faced with the fact that purely electronic music is known through the single version. The multiple performances that, as we have seen, are available in almost all the other art-forms, whether temporal or spatial, may well be the source of their constant self-renewal. If this is so, then every purely electronic composition may prove to be as intolerable in repetition as all movies, no matter how "artistic," seem eventually to become. (How many viewings of the greatest of movies—or of your own favorite—can you stand?) The absolute temporal control possible and necessary in these media permanently fixes our rate of scansion of the art objects; and it is this, I think, more than anything else, that ultimately deadens our response to them. For connoisseur and dilettante alike, they seem to pall relatively quickly; and what fails to hold the attention of the individual tends, in spite of the continuous supply of new audiences, to drop out of circulation altogether. Such a prediction, of course, is meant in no way as a reflection on the viability of the electronic medium; it merely throws doubt on the eventual survival of any individual work.

To be sure, electronic composers are by no means motivated by a desire to rid the world of performers (or, at least, not all of them are so motivated). Musical materials have become so complicated that in many cases electronic realization is now the only one possible, or the only one that can reproduce the composer's musical image with reasonable accuracy. After all, the more complex any musical dimension becomes, the fewer liberties of interpretation it permits. The purposely simple lines of a Handel aria allow more improvised variation than the ornamented lines of Bach, and with the increased complexity of nineteenth-century harmony improvisation tends to disappear altogether. In the same way, the rubato appropriate to a melodic composition of simple texture might prove impossible in a highly polyphonic work. Today such dimensions as dynamics and timbre are trying to achieve the complexity and precision of structure long enjoyed by the others, which in turn are moving to ever more advanced levels of organization. Even the most carefully and skillfully orchestrated composition of the past is still recognizable when transcribed, e.g. for piano, just as traditional paintings preserve many of their values when reproduced without color. But some composers are now moving in the direction of composing with tone-colors to the extent that their works will be as little susceptible of transcription as, say, "op" art is of black-and-white reproduction. A variation of timbre or of dynamics might constitute a "wrong note" comparable to an error in pitch. When one realizes that the same composers are often investigating the use of microtonal or other non-standard scales and of arithmetically intricate temporal ratios, it is easy to understand why music so put together would demand, not "interpretation," but maximum accuracy of every detail—an impossibility in the case of fallible human performance.

Happily, for those of us who enjoy playing and singing, some of the music of the past is still very much alive; and in spite of the proponents of aleatory and improvisatory and other forms of music that tend to diminish the roles of composer and performer alike, there is a good deal of non-electronic music being written today to which old-fashioned standards of good performance still apply. And even though the ideal performance may be a chimera, some performances are, after all, better than others. Some are superlative, and some are unacceptable. Although we can never achieve perfection (and indeed, if I am right, perfection in this area is a meaningless concept), we must still do the best we can.

Let us return, then, to the criterion previously put forward: that valid performance depends primarily on the perception and communication of the rhythmic life of a composition. That is to say, we must first discover the rhythmic shape of a piece—which is what is meant by its form—and then try to make it as clear as possible to our listeners. I have already tried to show how certain general rhythmic principles underly common formal units—the phrase, the period, the three-part song-form; and I have suggested that the same principles, working on higher levels and more comprehensive formal sections, can ultimately be invoked to explain an entire composition as one all-embracing rhythmic impulse. Such a comprehensive form can be made clear in performance, however, only by virtue of another principle: that the whole is more important than any of its parts. Any conflict of interest must be resolved by suppressing the formal claims of the part in favor of those of the whole.

Chopin's A major Prelude offers a short but instructive example. (There is, to be sure, some evidence that it should not be regarded as a complete composition, but as one

among twenty-four movements. If so, its performance in context might well differ from the one that will arise from our assumption of its independence. With this warning, however, let us proceed.)

In this little piece of sixteen measures, each pair of 3/4 measures is bound so closely together that we really hear eight hypermeasures of 6/4 (each, of course, beginning with an upbeat). This meter is so consistently supported by the motivic structure that toward the end, when the second measure is given additional stress, we hear it as a syncopation within the 6/4 rather than as a metrical shift. The obvious two-by-two balance of these motivic hypermeasures might tempt us to continue this combination on still higher levels, arriving at a uniform pattern. But any such trial—whether based consistently on the strong-weak organization of the hypermeasure, or reversing it at higher levels—is bound to show, perhaps even more clearly than the Mozart theme, the shortcoming of all attempts to invoke mechanically at higher levels the metrical arrangement of beats within a measure (or of measures within a hypermeasure). The resulting pattern, since it is indefinitely repeatable, fails to support the other aspects of musical form, for it contributes nothing to the progress of the piece toward its goal. This is why meter, as I have suggested, must yield to a more organic rhythmic principle.

We should look more closely, then, at the other musical elements and try to uncover the rhythmic form that they imply. The crescendo in mm. 11–12, together with the melodic climax and the harmonic complication at that point, might tempt us to make that pair of measures, or perhaps the next pair, strong, but we should resist. These measures are harmonically the most active of the entire piece; to make one of them a rhythmic goal through downbeat status would break the V–I–VI–II–V–I motion. Let us rather follow the hint the composer has given us through the parallelism of mm. 1–2 and 9–10, and divide the piece into two similar phrases. Now, as in the case of the Mozart theme, we can give each phrase its initial and cadential downbeats, and we can relate the two phrases as antecedent and consequent. The register of the bass also supports this picture. (The initial of each phrase—as of each hypermeasure—has an upbeat, just as each cadence is feminine; but I have omitted these details in order to simplify the diagram.)

mm. 1-2 3-4 5-6 7-8 9-10 11-12 13-14 15-16

But what worked so well in the case of the Mozart seems to fail here. The phrases are too similar, since each proceeds twice from dominant to tonic. And although the first phrase does not arrive at a perfect cadence, it nevertheless marks too firm a close too early in the piece. Thus, by allowing independence to each phrase, we have failed to produce a unified whole.

In order to discover what the shape of this whole should be, let us analyze the controlling melodic and harmonic line. This example (in which each notated measure represents one 6/4 hypermeasure) shows how I hear it:

Further simplification of each half leads to the following:

But this indicates that the whole can be heard as an augmentation of the second half—or rather, the second half as a diminution embedded within the whole! Now, this relationship can be brought out by emphasizing those hypermeasures that most clearly express the line, namely Nos. 1, 4, 5, and 8. Within each phrase, then, we still have our pattern ⌣ ⌣ ⌣ ⌣ . But at the next level, if we wish to make the augmentation as clear as possible, we must preserve the same pattern for the whole. This will mean underplaying both the cadence of the antecedent and the initial of the consequent. For the entire composition, then, we have:

$$| \underset{1 \quad 2}{\frown\smile} | \underset{3 \quad 4}{\smile -} | \underset{5 \quad 6}{-\smile} | \underset{7 \quad 8}{\smile\frown} |$$

(It may be purely coincidental that, according to the foregoing analysis, the two halves of the Prelude turn out to be transposed retrogrades of each other. But this relationship does further confirm the final rhythmic picture!)

Note once more that the positions of the strong measures are not necessarily determined by dynamic markings. Here, as almost always, linear and harmonic considerations take precedence. The arrival of a strong measure in such a case must be heralded by careful temporal adjustment rather than by simple accentuation. A further complication is now caused by the occurrence of units (such as hypermeasure 4) that are strong in their local context but belong to a group that becomes weak at the higher level. This is, of course, a result of the subordination of the demands of the individual phrase to those of the form as a whole. Indeed, such is the unifying effect of the weakening of the antecedent cadence and of the consequent initial downbeat that we are in fact no longer playing this piece as two balanced phrases, but as a single long one.

Naturally, in other contexts, other modifications of the individual members provide appropriate ways of binding phrase-groups into tighter units. In eight-measure periods, for example, if the break caused by the two consecutive strong measures 4 and 5 seems excessive, it will often be found that one of the following readings is suggested by the phrase-structure: | ⌢ ⌣ ⌣ − ⋮ ⌣ − ⌣ ⌍ | or | ⌢ ⌣ − ⌣ ⋮ − ⌣ ⌣ ⌍ | . (For the former, cf. Beethoven, Piano Sonata, Op. 13, Adagio, mm. 1–8; for the latter, his Piano Sonata, Op. 90, Rondo, mm. 1–8). The eight-measure sentence—as the 2+2+4 a–a–b pattern is sometimes called to distinguish it from the bipartite period —parallels, on a larger scale, a form we have already seen in the first phrase of the Mozart theme. It thus often suggests a corresponding reading on two levels. (Cf. Beethoven, Piano Sonata, Op. 2, No. 3, opening Allegro, mm. 1–8.)

The problem dimly raising its ugly head in the middle of the Chopin Prelude was that of premature closure: the creation of an impression of finality too early in a piece, usually through a perfect cadence in the tonic key. In this case the cadence was not perfect, but it was authentic; and the danger of closure was real enough to impel us to take steps to obviate it. In the Mozart example, on the other hand, we found perfect cadences both at the end of the first period and at the end of the entire theme. Here, however, both cadences were structurally feminine—unlike those of Chopin, which were feminine in detail only (since the bass entered on the first beat of a hypermeasure). Furthermore, the last Mozart cadence left an important melodic line (rising to the sixth degree) unresolved. If we look into the variations that follow, we find diverse ways of exploiting and developing both these features; but only with the coda is the line brought down to the tonic with a masculine cadence. (Note that the true measures of this coda are at variance with the notated ones. A more accurately written version would probably combine the last complete measure of the Allegro variation with the first half of the one following as a single measure of 3/2. Continuation in 4/4 would then bring the coda into proper metrical focus; see the example on p. 44.)

Mozart's compositional technique thus supports the principle of performance we applied to the Chopin Prelude: when premature closure threatens, try to avoid it by lightening the cadence. Even a masculine perfect cadence can

often be played in such a way as to sound structurally feminine—by placing the cadential accent on the measure preceding the final tonic. This kind of performance emphasizes the fact that the melodic descent to the tonic is, in such a position, only a local detail, and that the true line remains unresolved in order to make its definitive descent later on. There are, of course, many cases where the accentual adjustment is unnecessary—as when an elision begins a new section concurrently with the end of the old, or when a transitional upbeat borrows some of the time necessary for the finality of the full cadence. Yet there are many examples where closure can be postponed only in some such way. In the classical minuet, for example, if the minuet proper were played the first time as structurally feminine, and after the trio as masculine, the whole would achieve a unity otherwise lacking. One can extend this principle even further, provided it is not taken too literally. After all, one test of a good performance is the extent to which the listener knows where he is, even in a work with which he is unfamiliar. One good clue to such orientation could be the relative strength of the cadences—lighter toward the beginning, when the feeling of propulsion should be stronger than the sense of arrival, and heavier toward the end, as the goals become increasingly important. Even in the case of movements that seem to remain incorrigibly feminine, some differentiation can still be made. In the case of Chopin's Polonaise in A major, for example, a clever emphasis on one of the concealed cross-rhythms at the cadence can make the last chord sound, if not precisely masculine, at least like a strong tonic postponed by a suspension of the entire dominant.

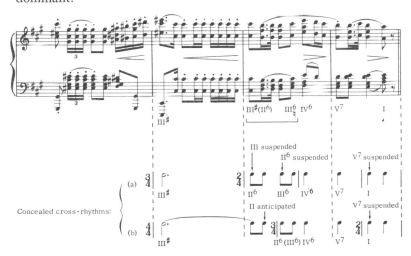

The foregoing discussion has touched on one aspect of a more general problem, viz., what to do about literal repetition. In specific instances this often assumes the aspect of a kind of Gordian knot, which can be untied only by Alexandrian methods—that is, by cutting. But at this point I should like to interject another of my foolish questions: Is there such a thing as literal repetition in music? I mean to imply nothing so profound as the Heraclitan impossibility of stepping into the same river twice, nor anything so trivial as the obvious fact that one can never play the same passage twice exactly alike. I can explain what I mean most easily by an example, for which let us return to the Chopin Polonaise. This is a piece notable for the six-fold statement of its opening period, each time literally repeated: AABABA, Trio, ABA—thus six A's in all. But the second A is already different from the first. The first was preceded by silence and followed by its repetition; the second is preceded by the first and followed by B. The third is now preceded and followed by B, and the fourth is preceded by B but followed by the Trio; and so on. My contention is that each statement is influenced by its position, by what precedes and what follows it, so that each is, in important respects, different from all the others.

In general, there is no such thing as true redundancy in music. In the case of a reiterated motif, for instance, we cannot say, "Now we get the point, so let's have something different." The point lies precisely in the fact that we get nothing different, but rather another repetition, and another, and still another, and yet another. (To take an example from a verbal medium, compare the cumulative effect of King Lear's "Never, never, never, never, never!") It is true, of course, that there are psychological and esthetic limits to the amount of repetition allowable. What is at first effective soon becomes comical and eventually boring. (Try adding a few more "nevers" to Lear's line.) It is only at this point that we can speak of redundancy—when each additional statement adds nothing new. Here, of course, we are once again facing Satie's wallpaper—and some of Warhol's movies.

From the performer's point of view, the practical problem arises when he is faced with the decision whether or not to make a repeat that seems purely conventional. But how often are such repeats purely conventional? Why, for example, was Beethoven so insistent that the exposition of the *Eroica* should be repeated? In this and similar instances, one can often adduce a number of reasons, any one of which would be sufficient to explain such a stance.

In the first place, in the case of a new work, a repetition of the exposition gives the audience another opportunity of absorbing its material. Such a consideration is no longer valid for Beethoven symphonies, but it might well have proved crucial for the comprehension of their early performances.

Much more important today is the question of proportions. Look at the first movement of Beethoven's Fifth Symphony. It is so short that there can be no excuse for suppressing the repeat; yet this is often done—with adverse effect. Its four sections—exposition, development, recapitulation, and coda—are so nearly the same length that the focus of the movement is blurred by the simple alternation of equal parts: statement–development–statement–development (for the coda is, of course, a second development). The repetition of the exposition effects the needed balance by strengthening the expository sections: AABAC.

A point that often seems insignificant, but is by no means always so, concerns the frequent appearance of a transitional return as a first ending. Even the few measures in this position in the *Eroica* are too good to miss. How much more important is the first ending of Mendelssohn's *Italian* Symphony. Here the composer introduces a new theme, one to which he will not again advert until the coda. Suppression of the first ending ruins the intended formal effect.

Even where there is no such transition, the differences of harmonic progression between returning and going on are often so striking as to suggest that this contrast is intentional on the part of the composer and essential to the design. A simple example is to be found in Beethoven's early Sonata in C minor, Op. 10, No. 1. The sudden opening of the development in C major, after the closing theme in E-flat, is a violent tonal wrench that, in the context, can be justified only by contrast with the more normal connection of E-flat with C minor afforded by a return to the beginning. A more sophisticated and problematic example is the corresponding point in the opening movement of Chopin's B-flat minor Sonata. Here the return itself creates a surprising deceptive resolution—but it is less surprising and more normal than the resolution leading into the development.[2]

Probably the most general possible justification for conventional repetitions of this kind is the new light they throw on old material. This principle works at its most obvious in the binary form of the suite, which is after all a progenitor of the repetition pattern of the sonata form. If we divide the musical material of a suite movement into Theme and Cadence, the standard pattern for major keys looks like this:

$$\lVert\text{:} \quad \underset{\text{I}}{\text{Theme—Cadence}} \quad \text{:}\lVert\text{:} \quad \underset{\text{V}}{\text{Theme—Cadence}} \quad \text{:}\rVert$$
$$\phantom{xxxx} \text{I} \phantom{xxxxxx} \text{V} \phantom{xxxxxxx} \text{V} \phantom{xxxxxxx} \text{I}$$

Observation of all indicated repeats will relate Cadence to Theme in three different ways: Cadence in V immediately followed by Theme in I, Cadence in V continued in the same key, and Cadence in I followed by Theme in V.

Fluctuating harmonic relationships like the above can of course be reflected in subtle variations of performance. Indeed, it would be a very simple movement altogether that did not admit of some kind of re-interpretation during the repetitions of its parts. Instead of deploring them as relics of an out-dated convention, we should welcome them as op-

[2] See Leonard Marcus, *A Musical Mutilation*, in *The Juilliard Review*, IV/3 (Fall, 1957), 6–16, for a discussion of this point with some well-chosen examples.

portunities for re-examination of musical material—just as
Baroque performers rejoiced in them as occasions for new
ornamentation. The six-fold statement in the Chopin Polonaise that initiated this discussion should thus be regarded
as a challenge rather than a chore. Theoretically, it might
even be feasible to play the piece in such a way as to make
each performance of the theme so characteristic of its specific role that an acute listener, hearing it out of context,
could identify its position in the whole.

The possibility of so many alternate readings for a single
section may raise certain doubts. At some point do we not
find that we are no longer achieving a performance grow-
ing out of a musical structure, but an "interpretation" more
or less arbitrarily applied to it? Certainly the pursuit of
variety for variety's sake exposes us to this danger, and for
this reason we must always be clear as to our purpose in
adopting diverse readings. Not only must each varied repetition be consistent with the composer's expressed formal
intentions and directions for performance, but it must also
be specifically justified by some complexity in the score that
it clarifies.

In determining just how such distinctions should be
made, the performer must again carefully consider the
rhythmic shape of the composition, and of its parts. The
second Brahms Waltz, Op. 39, a miniature song form that
also suggests a tiny sonata form, can serve as a compact
example. The first eight measures complete a tonicization of
the dominant, B. If we are returning to the opening tonic,
we shall not wish this to be heard as a true modulation;
hence we shall underplay the cadence, making it feminine
by bringing the cadential downbeat on the penultimate
measure. The second time through, in order to establish the
dominant more securely, we shall postpone the downbeat
until the final measure. As a result, the first time the dominant will lead easily back to the initial tonic; the second
time it will sound like a true point of arrival. (Because of
the crescendo to the last measure indicated both times, this

distinction must be made by temporal adjustment—e.g. by slightly delaying the last measure the second time.) It is more difficult in the second half of the piece to prevent the tonic cadence at the end from sounding too final the first time. Here again we should play it as feminine; and we should bring out the rising line in the bass, spanning the last two measures and connecting them with the opening of the section (A in the example). The second time, this line can be broken by a slight pause at the high point created by the $II^6$ in the middle of the penultimate measure; the descent to the final tonic in the bass can now be used to effect a masculine ending (B in the example).

Often a cadential phrase, confirming the key of a section, can similarly be read in two ways. In the Adagio of Haydn's Sonata in E minor (No. 34, formerly No. 2) the dominant, D, is established by a cadence in m. 18, but this is followed by almost three measures of confirmation. If this little phrase is played as a feminine tag to the tonicized D of m. 18, it prepares neatly for a return to the true tonic of the repeated exposition. But the same measures can be played with a crescendo to the final D, which converts m. 20 into the goal of the entire section. This masculine version in turn makes the sudden change of key of the ensuing development especially effective. Here the first two measures—the only appearance of the initial motif as a dominant—serve as an upbeat to the E minor statement that follows.

The same kind of adjustment, planned on a larger scale, can be applied to full-length sonata forms, so that even the repetition of the development-*cum*-recapitulation need not seem redundant. Mozart's Piano Sonata in A minor (K. 310) exhibits the following common key-structure: I–III in the exposition, III–V♯ in the development, and I–I (remaining in minor) in the recapitulation. Exposition and recapitulation end with similar five-measure phrases, each twice elaborating a simple I–II$^6_5$–V–I cadence in the appropriate key. Because of this circular nature, it is easy to play each phrase either as an expansion of its first chord (which, being approached as an elision from the preceding phrase, can be heard as strong), or as leading to its final tonic (which, by virtue of its position in the phrase and its pianistic layout, can equally well be heard as strong). In other words, the cadences of both exposition and recapitulation easily admit of both masculine and feminine interpretations. If one now wishes to make the indicated repeats, one can signal one's intention each time by the feminine version, which will smooth the connections III–I (from the end of the exposition back to the beginning) and I–III (from the end of the recapitulation to the beginning of the development). The second time through the exposition, a strong ending on III will clinch that key for its continuation into the development; and of course a masculine cadence at the end of the second recapitulation will rhythmically confirm the final tonic. (See example on facing page. It should be pointed out that the phrase in question is each time the last of three phrases, all cadentially affirming the local tonic. Adjustments of weight among these phrases could afford yet another means of distinguishing the two readings.)

From a purely practical point of view, of course, the decision whether to include or to suppress a specific repetition must depend on the exigencies of each occasion. The first ending of the opening Moderato of Schubert's B-flat Sonata contains material heard nowhere else in the movement, and the contrast of its harmonic directness is needed to justify the striking modulation that constitutes the second ending. Yet who would be bold enough to repeat this

A. End of exposition

B. End of recapitulation

exposition in a public recital?

Today we are likely to be impatient with all repetition, both in composition and in performance. Because of our own attempts to create a music of continuous mutation, we suspiciously scrutinize even the classics for traces of tautology. We tend to forget that, of all artistic effects, novelty is bound to be the least permanent. We are somewhat in the position of Mr. Gall, in Peacock's *Headlong Hall.* Said he, in reference to landscape architecture: "I distinguish the picturesque and the beautiful, and I add to them, in the laying out of grounds, a third and distinct character, which I call *unexpectedness.*" To which Mr. Milestone rejoined: "Pray, sir, by what name do you distinguish this character, when a person walks round the grounds for the second time?"

This exchange becomes apposite when we realize that, in one sense, internal repetition is only another form of what confronts us whenever we hear a familiar work yet another time. In both cases we are walking round the grounds for a second time.

Mr. Milestone has been well answered, for drama at least, by F. L. Lucas, whose remarks, with a little modification, are applicable to music as well: "Surprise may in general be left to melodrama and some kinds of comedy; Tragedy has in her quiver two more keenly pointed shafts than this: Suspense and Tragic Irony. From both we get an effect which is not exhausted in a flash and which is not staled by age. To the nervous person in the inn it is not the shoe dropped carelessly in the next room that is a source of agony, but the suspense of waiting for the second shoe to drop," [3] Suspense here means, not wondering what will happen, but waiting for what we know must happen. It affords us not only agony but also pleasure, or perhaps the two in an inextricably paradoxical marriage. Applying the principle to music, we can understand why, no matter how many times we hear the *Eroica,* the moment before the recapitu-

[3] F. L. Lucas, *Tragedy, Serious Drama in Relation to Aristotle's Poetics,* rev. ed., London: The Hogarth Press, 1957, p. 106.

lation never loses its effect. Indeed, the better we know the piece, the more inevitable, and therefore the more satisfying, the resolution seems to us.

Probably there is no such thing in music as true inevitability, short of the final cadence. (The analyst who insists that there is should be challenged by being asked to deduce the whole of an unfamiliar classic from its exposition—or even from its exposition plus development. Or perhaps he should be tested on the alternative versions of the same composition sometimes offered by certain composers, e.g. Liszt. Can the revision always be justified as more "inevitable" than the original?) Nevertheless, one test of a good composition is that repeated hearings build up in the listener an illusion of inevitability that is heightened by increased familiarity.

Lucas goes on to point out that "where surprise effects are greatly conceived, they may continue to be effective as suspense effects." [4] That is to say, if I may combine our two authors in one metaphorical mixture, when we walk round the grounds a second time we wait for that second shoe to drop. We can observe this principle in even such a simple (and hardly "greatly conceived") instance as the "surprise" chord in Haydn's Symphony No. 94. It may be one reason why, in well-composed music, deceptive cadences and sudden distant modulations never lose their power to startle. But there is often another factor at work here, and this one depends on the performer. Even in a piece we know by heart, a good performer can deceive us by the cadence and surprise us by the modulation. The convincing performance is one that absorbs the listener so deeply into the flow of the music that, even though he may know perfectly everything that lies ahead, he can still savor each moment as if for the first time.

Sessions puts it thus: "The listener . . . will respond to the musical gesture only as long as it strikes him freshly, or as long as he is capable of apprehending it as created anew

4 *Ibid.*, p. 106.

and not as something mechanically repeated. The agent of this re-creation is the imagination of the performer." [5] And again, "If music consists in movement, or what I have called inner gesture, it is the performer who supplies the impulse and the energy through which the movement and gesture as conceived in the composer's imagination is given concrete form. . . . The more truly he is able, in these terms, to engage himself completely in the music, to bring to it his own feeling for rhythm and movement, the more vital will be the performance." [6]

It is just as well, then, that there can be no such thing as an ideal interpretation. For if there were, we might long ago have ceased listening to Mozart and Beethoven. It is the renewed vitality of each performance that keeps them alive.

[5] *Op. cit.*, pp. 77-78.
[6] *Ibid.*, p. 84.

# III

))✦))✦))✦))✦))✦))✦))✦))✦))✦))✦

# THE PICTURE GALLERY

## Form and Style

Style, according to Whitehead, is "the ultimate morality of mind."[1] If this be so, then the comprehension and communication of musical style may well be the ultimate morality of performance—that is to say, its final responsibility. We all used to have a somewhat hazy notion about musical styles and their relation to performance, although we thought this was clearer than it actually was. Bach must be played straightforwardly; Beethoven, passionately; Chopin, with rubato. Mozart must be played Classically; Schumann, Romantically; and so on. What these generalities amounted to was usually no more than an indication that some composers should be played with more "freedom" than others, with the appropriate freedom increasing through the years in an almost unbroken line from Bach through Debussy, until Stravinsky suddenly broke the continuity with his insistence on absolute strictness. A more

[1] Alfred North Whitehead, *The Aims of Education,* New York: The Macmillan Co., 1929, p. 19.

sophisticated historical awareness has now shown us how superficial and even false such a view of musical style was. We know about the rhythmic licenses allowable in Bach, about Mozart's rubato, and about Chopin's demand for metric exactitude. Now we go so far in our attempts to reconstruct historically correct interpretations that we often lose the music itself. We forget that, until very recently, composition and performance were almost inseparable, that the present-day concept of interpretation as an independent subject of study and an art in itself is comparatively new and often entirely misleading. Besides, the rules of performance of the past were never meant to be applied in a restrictive way. They were never meant to be *applied* at all: they were—so far as they existed—merely expressions of the necessary relationship between the musical form and its physical expression. To take them more literally than that today is to misread them.

Ideally, any complete musical style should unequivocally imply its appropriate performance. By "complete style" I mean one that interrelates in an all-embracing unity every aspect of musical composition: tempo, meter, rhythm, melody, harmony, form. There is still, even in our historically conscious age, a great deal of confusion on this point. We speak of "The Fugue," as if a fugue by Beethoven had more than superficial points in common with one by Bach or one by Stravinsky. A description of *Ionisation* states that it is in sonata form, without questioning what sonata form can possibly mean in music lacking pitch structure.[2] Form is an essential aspect of style—indeed, it should summarize all aspects of a style. When this is not the case, the style is accordingly incompletely realized—a criticism that, as we shall see, can be applied to some phases of nineteenth-century Romanticism.

Style characteristics are seen most clearly in comparisons and contrasts. Confronted by a single picture, we may not

[2] See Nicolas Slonimsky, *Music Since 1900*, 3rd ed., New York: Coleman-Ross Co., Inc., 1949, p. 340.

be sure whether it is a Rembrandt or a Maes; in a gallery, side by side with other works of the two masters, it may proclaim its identity unmistakably (even in one of those un-friendly galleries that refuse to label their possessions). What I propose, therefore, is a short walk through a museum where we can compare and contrast the features of those musical styles most familiar to us. We shall begin in the room marked Late Baroque, go on (skipping a small one in between variously labelled Rococo, Galant, etc.) to the one marked Classical, proceed to the one called Romantic, and end with a brief look at the Late Romantic, with perhaps a glimpse through the door into Modern. It will be impossi-ble, of course, to examine each period in all its details; so I propose to concentrate on those aspects of rhythm and de-sign that influence performance most obviously.

Certainly the style of our first period, the age of Bach and Handel, is most memorably characterized by an im-portant rhythmic feature: the uniformity of its metrical pulse. This is in turn but one facet of a regularity that per-vades the texture of the music. As a result the typical move-ment of this period is indeed a *movement,* i.e. a piece composed in a single unvarying tempo. To be sure, there are the exceptions duly labelled as fantasias; yet the rule remains that each tempo should be represented by an extended, relatively self-contained unit. Even when a move-ment juxtaposes two or more such units in clearly con-trasted tempos, there is often an underlying arithmetical relation that, if observed in performance, unifies them. (See, for example, Arthur Mendel's analysis of Bach's *St. Anne* Fugue.[3]) In this music, events of the same kind tend to happen either at the same rate of speed, or at pre-cisely geared changes of rate, whether these events are cycles of keys, short-range harmonic progressions, or se-quences of melodic motifs. In the best of this music, the contrapuntal texture, either actual or implied, sets up a

[3] Arthur Mendel, *A Note on Proportional Relationships in Bach Tempi,* in *The Musical Times,* No. 1402 (Dec. 1959), 683–85.

hierarchy of events, each proceeding at its own rate, yet all under a strict metric control that extends from the entire phrase down to the smallest subdivision of the beat.

Look for example at the episode that begins at m. 28 of the opening Allegro of Bach's D minor Clavier Concerto. (See the music example on the preceding pages which, for reasons to be explained later, begins with m. 26.) Six measures here (mm. 28-33) form an area of relative uniformity, since they consist of a two-measure model followed by two sequences; this is the over-all pattern of the little passage. In turn, each two-measure group is articulated as a pair by the regular imitation between the first and second violins. This device imposes a measure-by-measure circle of fifths on the larger harmonic motion. Within each measure, the two-fold division is continued by the motion of the bass, and the further division of each half-measure into quarters is indicated by the right-hand figure of the clavier. That this figure is not mere filler but is motivic is indicated by the two preceding measures in the clavier, which prepare the sixteenth-note arpeggio first in quarters and then in eighths, and also by the way the figure is extended at the end of each two-measure unit in order to prepare for the next.

We can go still further. The weak beats of each measure
are given special articulation by the viola, and the weak
half of each beat is brought out by the octave leap in the
left hand of the clavier, as well as by the implied inner
melody in the right hand (indicated by arrows in the
example). But even among these weak half-beats some
differentiation is made. Those of the first beat receive a
special accent by virtue of the principal violin motif (as
indicated by a presumably authentic staccato mark), and
the same motif confers a syncopation upon the weak half of
the third beat. Finally, we should note that, just as the passage was entered by means of a progressive diminution of
the clavier arpeggio, it is left by a diminution of the length
of the sequence (with its consequent effect of speeding
up): the continuation (mm. 34–39) reduces the sequence
first to one measure, then to one-half measure, before taking leave of it to arrive at a cadence.[4]

The same concept of metrical hierarchy can be called
upon to explain certain puzzling passages, among them the
famous twenty-third measure of the first Prelude in *The
Well-Tempered Clavier*. Which is chordal, the B or the C?
Is the measure to be heard as a diminished or an altered
supertonic seventh? The key lies in an analysis along the
lines already suggested. Each measure is, of course, divided
in two by exact reiteration; each quarter note is articulated
as either the lower or the upper extreme of the half-measure motif. But it is the eighth-note motion that will par-

[4] Since writing the above, I have been pleased to read a somewhat
similar analysis of Bach's rhythm by Henri Pousseur. See his *The
Question of Order in New Music*, in *Perspectives of New Music*, V/1
(Fall-Winter 1966), 95–96.

ticularly interest us. In spite of the internal repetition of the
last three sixteenths of the motif, every eighth note attacks
a different member of the chord, suggesting a basic four-
part harmony under the apparent five-voice texture; but at
the same time the cross-rhythm of $(2+3)+3$ or $2+(3+3)$
sixteenths prevents monotony. In performance, however,
the regular pattern should be brought out at the expense
of the cross-rhythm, which is motivically evident enough
without further emphasis.

If this reading is maintained, the measure in question will
reveal itself. Both chords can be heard—first the diminished
seventh, and then the supertonic. The composer has prepared for the long dominant pedal by here combining two
measures into one. The performer can indicate this by emphasizing the soprano during the first statement, but then
bringing out the inner-voice motion between B and C during the repetition (see example, top of p. 65). Perhaps this
measure, with its dual harmony, is one justification for the
persistent reduplicative design of the entire prelude.

In this connection it is important to realize that the B–C
relationship, which some might wish to dismiss as a mere
detail of voice-leading, was apparently in Bach's mind from
the earliest stages of the composition of this Prelude. It plays
a striking role, although in a different form, in the early

sketches (reproduced in Hans Bischoff's edition, now pub-
lished by Schirmer and Kalmus). One ought to note further
that in the Prelude No. 2 in C minor, likewise built on a
reduplicative design, the approach to the dominant pedal
is again heralded by a harmonic doubling-up within a mea-

sure, although of a different type. This time (m. 18) it is effected by a passing seventh in the bass. (What bearing analysis of the foregoing kind may have on a decision as to the precise instrument for which Bach was writing, or as to the relevance of the concept of *notes inégales* to the performance of this music, I leave to historians to consider.)

The motivic cross-rhythm mentioned above is a small example of the way metrical ambiguities are used to advantage to offset an otherwise unrelieved squareness. In triple meters the hemiola is frequent in cadences but by no means restricted to them. A longer-range ambiguity, strictly controlled and eventually resolved, is shown by the beginning of the concerto movement already examined. Although written in 2/2, the opening theme could also be heard in 3/2. This possibility is deliberately explored by the ensuing solo passage. Indeed, it is not until the episode previously analyzed that the duple meter is unambiguously established. At this point we can see that the composer has been playing with threes against the steady duple division of wholes into halves and halves into quarters. From the beginning we find in turn: a theme of 6 measures; a solo passage of the same length divided as 4 x 3 half-measures; the theme again, now 6+3 measures long; another 6–measure solo, this time ending with a suggestion of a 3/4 cross-rhythm (m. 27); now our episode, which turns out to consist of 3 x 2, plus 3 x 1, plus 3 x ½ measures, with a cadence of 1½ measures (see example on following pages).

We can best understand such metric play if we assume that in this style the primary metric unit is not the measure but the beat—in this case the half or quarter note. This is not to say that the measure is unreal, or purely conventional; but it is only one step in the hierarchical subdivision and combination of beats, which remain the unchanging elements. (Even the Late Baroque is, after all, not so far away from the Renaissance!) In the entire movement we have been discussing, with the exception of the opening and closing unison statements, there is an attack on every

half note from beginning to end, even on every quarter. One finds similar consistency in the two remaining movements of the concerto. The beats seem to form a pre-existing framework that is independent of the musical events that it controls. One feels that before a note of the music was written, the beats were in place, regularly divided into appropriate sub-units, and regularly combined into measures; and that only after this abstract framework was in place, so to speak, was the music composed upon it. Sometimes the music fits the abstract measure precisely, sometimes not —witness not only the passages we have been discussing, but also the frequent displacements undergone by fugue subjects, especially during strettos. But in every case the element common to both the framework and the musical substance is the beat.

In performance, the result should be a relative equalization of the beats. Our orientation within the measure should be effected more by the actual musical profile than by applied accentuation (which, after all, was unavailable on two of Bach's favorite instruments). The metrical ambiguities and shifts can thus express themselves naturally in accordance with the varying rhythmic context.

It is easy to see that a framework of such uniformity is a

natural background for the monothematic forms character-istic of the Baroque, or, conversely, that the monothematic forms are the natural expression of a style based on such consistent rhythmic premises. In fact, one should not even speak of monothematic forms but of one formal principle, which is the same whether embodied in the fugue, the con-certo, or the aria. The recurrent subject of a fugue functions in the same way as the *ritornello* of a concerto or of an aria —to confirm the establishment of an important key area in the tonal cycle. The fugal episodes, like the solo passages of the concerto or aria, in general move from one such area to the next. The steadiness of the motion through the keys, from tonic back to tonic, is reflected in the thematic recur-rences. And the tonal motion itself, by its apparent inexora-bility, seems to reflect the regular progression of beat to beat, measure to measure, phrase to phrase. This is, I sup-pose, what people mean when they talk loosely about the logic of Bach's musical designs: they are really referring to his utter consistency of style.

Recognition of the similarity of fugal episodes to solo passages will guard one against playing them in accord-ance with the nonsense one sometimes reads about their "loose" or "subordinate" character.[5] In fact, they are often the passages of greatest tension, relieved only by the simul-taneous arrival of a stable key and a subject. Oddly enough, the thoroughgoing stretto–fugue may reverse this effect. The strettos usually create tension, which is resolved by single statements or free cadences. (Need it be pointed out, in this connection, that when the strettos involve augmentation or diminution, they embody thematically the principles of metric hierarchy that are basic to the style?)

It is in the metric realm that we find what is probably the most striking point of contrast between the Late Baroque

5 "The episodes, although still in strict counterpoint, are somewhat 'lighter weight' and stand to the preceding expositions in the relation-ship of relaxation to tension." From the entry on "Fugue" in the *Harvard Dictionary & Music*, ed. Willi Apel; Cambridge, Mass.: Harvard University Press, 1945, p. 285.

and Classical styles. Superficially, the Classical period appears to respect the fundamental pulse almost as wholeheartedly as the earlier period, for the typical Classical composition retains a single meter unchanged from beginning to end. But the pulse is seldom persistently obvious to our ears, and in fact the true pulse may change from one part of a movement to the next, even though the indicated meter remains the same. A movement in 4/4 may, for various themes or developments, move at a basic rate of a quarter, a half, or even a whole note. It will feel no compulsion whatsoever to mark every important beat by an attack. It may call upon syncopations to set up cross-rhythms much more drastic than those of the Baroque. And it is just here that we find the clue to the Classical approach to meter. Why do these cross-rhythms—say, those in the first movement of the *Eroica*—sound so powerful? Because they represent, not just an ambiguity, but a conflict. The rhythmic surface is here insistently at odds with the prevailing measure. For it is the measure, rather than the beat, that is the fundamental unit in Classical music. The measure was important in the previous style, too, but it was to be heard as a multiplication of the primary and all-powerful beat. The beat is important in the Classical style, but it is arrived at by subdivision of the measure. That is why the beat may vary so much from one part of a movement to another: the measure is being subjected to different forms of subdivision.

As a result, a Classical theme is tied more firmly to its metrical position. For this reason, intelligent performance demands a decision in every doubtful case as to what the real (as opposed to the notated) measure is. Normally, to be sure, the two coincide, but there are frequent exceptions. The extension or the elision of a cadence occasionally shifts a passage (even a thematic return) to the "wrong" half of a 4/4 measure. In most of these cases the true measure itself has been shifted, the composer not having felt it necessary (or conventionally allowable) to change the metric notation. Such shifts explain a number of puzzling passages that today would be clarified by notating a temporary change of meter. (We have encountered one at the end of the variations of Mozart's Sonata in A major, caused in this case by the elision of a cadence occurring in the middle of a measure.[6] ) The point is that the true measure is always there to be determined, and primary once it is.

It is significant that shorter measure-lengths come into more general use during this period: they provide for greater flexibility in grouping and obviate the occasional metrical contradictions that arise from the longer measures. (At the same time they create new problems. In very rapid tempos the measures become so short that they really function as beats, and it is not always clear just how they should be articulated. How do you read the strong and weak measures in the Scherzo of Beethoven's Piano Sonata, Op. 110? Do the accented measures of the coda represent downbeats or syncopations? Do you agree with Schnabel or with Tovey?)

The variation in pulse is an indication that, even within a single tempo, not all the parts of a movement progress at the same speed. It is this changing rate of progression, rather than multiplicity of musical subject-matter, that is basic to the bithematic or polythematic forms of the period. As we know, Haydn often uses the same material for both first and second subjects of a sonata-allegro; but in such cases a change in the harmonic rhythm can so alter the speed of the theme as to produce an entirely new effect. In the first movement of his Piano Sonata in E-flat (No. 49, formerly No. 3) the opening theme moves slowly: two full measures of tonic, a measure of transitional harmony, and a cadence on the dominant; then an answering phrase that proceeds in the same way from V back to I. In the second theme, the same motif is used to present the same I-V, V-I swing in the space of four measures.

[6] See also my discussion of a passage from Mozart's Piano Quartet in G minor, K. 478, in a communication to *Perspectives of New Music*, I/2 (Spring 1963), 206–10.

A. First theme

B. Second theme

The foregoing example shows us to what extent the rhythmic shape of this music depends on the actual musical content of each passage. Although by no means free of the metrical framework in the background, this shape is governed primarily by the motivic development in the foreground, and by the harmonic organization of the phrase. There is, in the best examples of this style, a balance between the demands of the abstract meter and those of the concrete rhythm that produces a uniquely satisfying effect. The music itself gives the effect of creating the meter that it requires for its own existence.

One sometimes hears remarks about the tyranny of the four-measure phrase during this period. It is true that the four-measure phrase—or rather some sort of parallel balance—can usually be felt as a norm; but it is never, in the music of the masters, a tyrant. This is because it is for them a rhythmic, not a metric entity. Conceived metrically it would tend to become as fixed and invariable as the measure; conceived rhythmically, it is as flexible as the musical surface itself. The contrast between the two Haydn themes is one example; the Mozart theme previously analyzed is another. One more instance, this time from Beethoven—the opening of his Piano Sonata, Op. 2, No. 1—will further indicate the variety of ways in which the motivic and harmonic development of the phrase creates its unique form.

The entire phrase of eight measures naturally divides into 2+2+4. An examination of the motivic structure of the second half finds a reduced pattern of 1+1+2. (A similar relationship was exhibited by the Mozart example.) A linear analysis of the ascending melody supports this motivic division, for it can be heard thus: two measures of F, two measures of G, one of A-flat, one of B-flat, and two of an extended C. But now a look at the bass discovers, beginning in the fifth measure, an exact diminution of this accent! The result is that the harmony shows a steady increase in speed until the cadential measure:[7]

| 𝅝—𝅗𝅥 | 𝅝—𝅗𝅥 | 𝅝 | 𝅝 | 𝅗𝅥 𝅗𝅥 | 𝅝 ‖

Thus these eight measures, which superficially fall into the conventional sentence-pattern, are actually bound together in a tightly unified progression. If one looks a little further, at the answering phrase, one finds that it begins conventionally, as if it might parallel the opening eight measures. But its development is completely different, being based on the isolation and expansion of its second measure, and its eight measures are expanded to twelve.

The formal design that is ideal for the Classical style, as the fugal or ritornello design was for the Baroque, is of course the sonata-allegro. One can trace how, during this period, other patterns, from compact song forms to extended rondos, aspire to the sonata—how dominant cadences tend to return in the tonic, how central episodes expand into developments, and so on. It is easy to see that the Classical style, with its possibilities of rhythmic variety, is admirably adapted to polythematic forms, and to the kind of treatment that typifies the development section. But more important than the form as a pattern is the unifying principle behind it, which, I believe, is not to be found in its bithematicism, or its developmental aspect, or its binary or ternary (take your choice!) structure. Let us recall for a moment that the principle underlying both the fugue and the concerto was the recurrence of the theme at every important point of harmonic arrival. The corresponding principle for the Classical style—let us call it the sonata

[7] Erwin Ratz carries the harmonic speed-up still further by analyzing the last measure as implying two harmonies, each a quarter-note long. See his *Einführung in die musikalische Formenlehre,* Vienna: Österreichischer Bundesverlag, 1957, p. 23.

principle for want of a better term—is somewhat more complex. It requires that important statements made in a key other than the tonic must either be re-stated in the tonic, or brought into a closer relation with the tonic, before the movement ends. Expressed thus, the principle covers many aspects of formal treatment. It applies, most obviously, to the role of the "second subject" in exposition and recapitulation. But it also explains why Beethoven takes such pains in the coda of the first movement of the *Eroica* to re-introduce the theme of the development, and in such a way as to modulate directly to the tonic. It suggests why Mozart sometimes introduces into the coda of a rondo the cadential tag from a central episode (as in the Andante of the Piano Concerto in E-flat, K. 482); and why Beethoven, in a similar position, sometimes makes a special bow to the key of such an episode, even though he may feel it unnecessary to mention its theme. (See, for example, the last movement of the *Sonata Pathétique*, Op. 13. Here, instead of referring to the theme of the central episode, the composer associates the opening theme with the key of the episode, which is at the same time brought into close relation with the tonic.) This interpretation of the sonata principle also clarifies the form of many of Mozart's operatic numbers (the Trio from Act I of *The Marriage of Figaro*, for example). Above all, it explains the cumulative effect of the form, which is the source of what many refer to as its dramatic power. For in a movement so constructed nothing is lost; everything that occurs will have its influence on the outcome and will have to be reckoned with before the piece is over.

If we view the sonata form in this way, we must realize that it is not so much the contrast between the themes as their ultimate *rapprochement* that is most striking. We can therefore understand why, during the Classical period, a general uniformity of tempo prevails during each movement despite the diversity of the events that it governs. True, a movement by Mozart or Beethoven can, or even should, sustain more freedom of tempo than one by Bach or Handel; but a single tempo should ideally prevail. Even the obvious exceptions are sometimes more apparent than real. The development and the coda of the opening movement of Beethoven's Piano Sonata, Op. 109 suggest, for example, that the Vivace and the Adagio are connected by an arithmetically exact proportion that equates a quarter note of the former with a sixteenth of the latter, or a measure of the Adagio with six of the Vivace. Although Beethoven, according to Schindler, felt that his music demanded frequent changes of tempo, the telling phrase is the qualification: "for the most part perceptible only to the sensitive ear".[8]

With Schubert, however, we find movements, apparently composed in a single tempo, for which we nevertheless can find no one speed that really works. We are now on the border of Romanticism; and wide tempo variation, whether implicit or explicit, is indeed characteristic of the later style. Chopin may mark numerous changes of tempo in the First Ballade, or almost none in the Fourth; yet to seek for a single governing tempo proves to be as fruitless in the latter case as in the former. Later composers give up the pretense completely—witness the symphonies of Tchaikovsky.

The tendency of the nineteenth century is increasingly to emphasize the forces of contrast over those of unification; and this applies not only to tempo but to thematic material, harmonic progression, rhythm, and mood. (The unifying power of thematic transformation is often more apparent than real, for the device may emphasize superficial relationships among sections that are basically disparate.) The principle of contrast obtains, too, not only within individual works, but among the works of one composer, and above all among composers. This is what makes the music of the Romantic period so hard to characterize neatly. Whatever further general statement one may make, there will always be at least one major composer who can be adduced in ref-

---

[8] Anton Schindler: *Biographie von Ludwig van Beethoven*, 4th ed., Münster: Aschendorff, 1871, part 2, p. 243, The specific reference here is to the Largo of the Piano Sonata, Op. 10, No. 3.

utation. (And there is always Berlioz!) Still, there are certain obvious points of difference between the music of this period and those preceding it, points having to do with the questions of rhythm and articulation that have been concerning us in the Baroque and Classical styles.

The metrical unit in Romantic music continues to be the measure, as it was in the Classical period; and the measures are combined into more or less regular phrases. Nevertheless, there has been a subtle but important change in orientation. In the Classical period, as we have seen, the measure was usually the largest metrical unit. Its steadiness served as a constant support for—or counterpoint to—the variety of motif- and phrase-construction. When measures combined to form phrases, they did so not in any regular metrical way but as components of freely articulated rhythmic groups whose structure depended on their specific musical content. In Romantic music, on the other hand, one can find long stretches in which the measures combine into phrases that are themselves metrically conceived—into what I call hypermeasures. This is especially likely to occur whenever several measures in succession exhibit similarity of motivic, harmonic, and rhythmic construction. These al-most demand to be counted as units. The desire of the measure to behave as a single beat, already noticeable in very fast Beethoven scherzos, is here intensified—and not only in very fast tempos. As a result, the groupings are often irresistibly drawn into a regular four-measure pattern. It is here, and not in the preceding style, that we can justly speak of the tyranny of the four-measure phrase!

The best composers, to be sure, developed individual ways of coming to terms with the problem of the inevitably threatening monotony. Mendelssohn concealed the prevailing pattern by clever elisions, harmonic overlaps, and extensions. Schumann, of all the great men of the period, seemed to glory in the *Viertaktigkeit*. He was able to keep it going without relief throughout long sections by the systematic use of strong syncopations and cross-rhythms that have consequently become a hallmark of his style. The last movement of his Piano Concerto is a brilliant demonstration of how to write in long spans of four-measure units and at the same time make the result interesting by rhythmic ingenuity.

The composer who really absorbed, digested, assimilated, and nourished himself on the four-measure concept was Chopin. In his dances, and in movements derived from dance forms, the hypermeasures are obvious to the ear and sometimes overly persistent. Other compositions, however, exhibit the same pattern firmly in control, yet concealed with a subtlety that mitigates the hypermeter without violating it. For Chopin, the norm became so nearly instinctive that he could temper it with cross-rhythms and syncopations in the large, just as Schumann did in detail. A familiar example is the middle section of the Fantasy-Impromptu, where the apparent irregularities of phrasing are only details on the surface of a strict four-by-four design. More sophisticated treatment is to be found throughout the Polonaise-Fantasy, which in this respect is indeed a fantastic polonaise.

The effect on performance of the use of increasingly large metric units can be heard in an easy experiment. Take a few measures of keyboard passagework from Bach, from Mozart, and from Chopin.[9] Play each in its proper tempo and with its appropriate articulation; then try each with the tempo and articulation of each of the other two. In every case, you will find that what sounds natural on any one makes the others sound like finger exercises. The Bach figuration demands to be played metrically, i.e., with every beat and sub-beat clearly articulated. The Mozart must be played melodically, with attention to the motivic relationships that determine the rhythmic shape. The Chopin figuration, by contrast, is coloristic. Sweeping over huge areas,

[9] E.g.: Bach, Clavier Concerto in D minor, mm. 7–12; Mozart, Piano Concerto in A major, K.488, first movement, mm. 86–98; Chopin, Impromptu in F-sharp major, mm. 82–100.

it is distinguished more by its contours and by its over-all sound than by its structural details. Least of all the three does it submit to metrical subdivision.

It is not until late in the century that the rhythmic problem becomes really acute. Then metric uniformity is allied with a related tendency of the period in such a way that the two exacerbate each other. I refer to the habit of writing in sequences and quasi-sequences. Schubert had long ago exploited this device as a facile way of filling out transitions and developments. Some of his most successful development sections (e.g. that of the first movement of the Cello Quintet, Op. 163) are based on huge sequences; and at least one whole movement, the finale of the *Trout* Quintet, can be described as a model plus a single sequence based on it (I–IV, V–I)! Later composers, especially Liszt, use the same device for thematic construction. Even the impressive opening of *Vallée d'Obermann* loses some of its magic when we realize that it consists of only a model followed by a sequence a minor third higher. The same kind of treatment imparts a slightly mechanical atmosphere to some of Wagner's noblest pages.

What has happened, during the procession of styles from Late Baroque to Romantic, is that the focus of musical interest has, as it were, moved in the opposite direction to that of the metrical focus. We do not hear these sequences in the same way as those of earlier periods. When we listen to a Bach sequence (such as the one analyzed above), our attention is less on the material itself (which is, after all, thematically familiar at this point in the movement) than on the general direction of the entire passage. In hearing a typical sequence by Wagner or Liszt (say, the opening of *Obermann* just cited), we concentrate on the detail—on the content of each step rather than on the progression as a whole. Thus, as the basic metrical units have become larger and larger, the units of musical attention, so to speak, have diminished. It is in the Classical period that, as usual, we find a unique balance: detail and progression demand equal attention and prove equally rewarding.

Eventually, with Franck and Bruckner, the metrical units seem to have expanded to the point that one sometimes finds oneself tempted to count, not beats, not measures, but hypermeasures, i.e., the sequences themselves! (Excesses in this direction can be heard throughout the finale of Franck's String Quartet). At this point metric and hypermetric articulation have gone too far, and it is not surprising to find that with Strauss, Mahler, and especially Debussy, a new, looser, sometimes almost anti-metrical principle begins to emerge. The composers of the early twentieth century move in the direction of much freer rhythmic articulation, governed less by metric than by motivic considerations. For many later composers, abstract meter seems not even to exist: what meter there is expresses itself only through the actual rhythmic motifs of the musical surface and hence is in a state of constant flux. Inevitably, such a style lacks a tension that characterizes much music of the past. This may explain why Webern apparently insisted on the importance of his regular metric notation, in spite of its persistent contradiction of the rhythmic content of his scores.

Perhaps the chief reason why it is difficult to find a new unifying formal principle at work during the Romantic era, comparable to those of earlier periods, is the reverence in which the composers of the nineteenth century hold the Classical sonata—only viewed no longer as a principle but as a "form." For Mendelssohn and Brahms the older patterns prove adequate. Brahms, indeed, understands the Classical ideal so thoroughly that he is able to control the harmonic innovations of Schubert and later composers in forms almost as tight as those of Beethoven. Others, however, from Chopin to Bruckner and beyond, dutifully try, in individual ways, to force intractable material into an unyielding mould. Fortunately, many of them realize from time to time the essentially abstract and historically spurious nature of the framework they are seeking to impose on their ideas, and produce works—even large-scale ones—revealing new approaches to form.

Berlioz, at his most characteristic, experiments with what might be called a counterpoint of musical spaces, when he combines themes or reveals a stationary idea in constantly new guises by creating motion around it. Sometimes, as in his Requiem, the musical space is even translated into physical space.

There is a similar strain in Schumann, with his distant or interior voices counterpointed against the normal flow of the music. Sometimes, as during the unplayed melody of his *Humoresque*, this suggests the possibility of two simultaneous musical forms—the one to be heard by the audience and the other to be thought by the performer. In fact, there may even be a third form present, known only to the composer. This concept of multiple form may also explain those passages where Schumann's syncopations are so persistent that the listener cannot perceive the metrical background; such sections may present different, but equally intelligible, forms to performer and to audience. The same concept may explain similar difficulties in twentieth-century music, including, for example, Webern's cross-rhythms and his extraordinary notation in the Piano Variations of an empty measure of accelerando followed by a fermata.[10]

Chopin's early works display either a fundamental lack of comprehension of the sonata principle or a deliberate flouting of it; but of all the composers of the period he ultimately achieves the most personal and in some ways the most successful transformation of the form for his own purposes. I refer not only to the Fantasy and the last two Ballades, all openly based on modified sonata patterns, but to the Polonaise-Fantasy and the Barcarolle as well, which apply the sonata principle to forms derived elsewhere. In most of these works Chopin uses an important device that

[10] Webern is said to have meant this notation perfectly seriously. See Peter Stadlen, *Serialism Reconsidered*, in *The Score*, 22 (Feb. 1958), 15.

I somewhat extravagantly refer to as *apotheosis*: a special kind of recapitulation that reveals unexpected harmonic richness and textural excitement in a theme previously presented with a deliberately restricted harmonization and a relatively drab accompaniment. The clearest example is probably the reprise of the chief theme of the Polonaise-Fantasy (see example on page 85). This is Chopin's version of what, in Liszt and Wagner, becomes the thoroughgoing method of theme-transformation; and it is a clue to what finally emerges as a candidate for the Romantic form principle.

What this is can be deduced from an examination of Liszt's larger movements, whether extended sonata forms, or arch-forms (e.g. ABCBA), or a combination of the two. What is striking is his frequent unwillingness to recapitulate a theme without some important alteration. This is especially true of those occasions when it is necessary to bring back a theme in a key other than that in which it is first presented. One feels that, for Liszt, a given version of a theme belongs in only one key—and often at only one temporal point. The required change need not entail a thoroughgoing rhythmic or harmonic transformation: often a new accompaniment figure or a different instrumental layout is sufficient. But even this fact is symptomatic of a novel view of the nature of a theme. For the Classical composers, a theme was typically a complete melodic-harmonic-rhythmic-textural unity; for the Romantics, it is rather a melody capable of appearing in many varied harmonic, rhythmic, and textural garbs. (The distinction applies also to explicit variation forms, even though every variation is to some extent a transformation. The Classical composers use the form to examine or—especially in the case of Beethoven—to explore the theme; the Romantics tend to use the theme as a point of departure.)

The unique key-preferences of Romantic themes, and the various guises they assume when forced to change key, may be due in part to the instrumentally idiomatic way

A. Original version

many of them are conceived by their composers. Passage-work for piano, for example, may lie very awkwardly under the fingers when transposed—as any student knows who has worked on Chopin's Scherzo in C-sharp minor. This fact may help to explain Chopin's idiosyncratic treatment of key-relations in his concertos. With his later works the new principle begins to take over, notably in the Fourth Ballade, which presents its first theme in ever-new figurations, and apotheosizes the return of its second theme. Even with Schumann we find hints of a similar concept. The first movement of his Piano Concerto is a sonata-allegro, but it is one in which each successive key area is marked by a new version of the principal subject, until the exigencies of the recapitulation he considers obligatory force him to re-peat himself. Even then, the coda affords him one more op-portunity for a unique presentation. (It is interesting in this connection to see how Schumann, later, in his symphonies, sometimes compresses or bypasses the recapitulation in fa-vor of an expanded coda. Look at the finale of the Second Symphony, or at the first movement of the Fourth.)

It has often been remarked that, in the developed music-dramas of Wagner, important motifs belong to certain keys and are at home nowhere else. The "Sword" belongs in C, "Valhalla" in D-flat, and so on. The choice of such keys may again be influenced by the desire for orchestral effective-ness, but it is also at least partially governed by musico-dra-matic considerations. For when these motifs appear in new keys, they are usually transformed in some dramatically significant way. Exact recapitulation is in general so rare in Wagner as to excite curiosity as to its justification, and the same becomes true of Strauss in both tone-poem and opera. Are we not moving here toward a musical form of complete stream-of-consciousness, in which no exact recapitulation is possible because no two moments of our lives are ever alike? It is hardly a coincidence that the composer who argues most explicitly that music reproduces our inner life should produce a dramatic work notable for its apparently complete lack of recapitulation—*Erwartung*. One might say that in this monodrama every moment is represented by its own leitmotif.

We have thus moved from the Baroque point of view that a theme is equally at home everywhere, through the Classical desire to relate every theme to the tonic, to the principle that each theme belongs uniquely to one key and perhaps even to one statement. Whether those are right who now believe that the next step is to dispense with the theme entirely, it is probably too early to say. Even if they prove right for today, they have not answered the question for tomorrow. No artistic style—not even that of ancient Egypt—has ever proved permanent in the past, and it is highly unlikely that any will become so now or in the future. The direction of change, however, we cannot know, any more than we can predict the direction of history in general. We shall have to leave it to those in charge: the composers. It is they who must determine the course of stylistic evolution—and not by what they say or write about music, but by the music they write.

# ON TWO MODES OF

# ESTHETIC PERCEPTION

The foregoing essays may seem to rest on the implicit assumption that there is only one mode of perception by which we should properly experience works of art: namely, the *synoptic comprehension* of their structure. Certainly this mode has been awarded primacy in these pages, but it would be an error to assume it as the only possible or even the only appropriate one. Esthetic perception depends on at least one other mode, equally important. A clarification of the distinction between the two may be helpful in suggesting ways of balancing my intentionally one-sided presentation of the problems of musical performance. Although the discussion will necessarily involve some overlap with ideas already presented, I shall try to keep this redundancy to a minimum.

According to some writers, synoptic comprehension, which either recognizes a unity in what is perceived or else imposes one on it, is essential to the esthetic experience. Stein implies as much by relating that experience exclusively to the esthetic object, which "has three properties—it is *known*; it is *unified*; it *endures*, that is, it is not consumed by use."[1] But "esthetic," as I wish to define the word, applies to *any* perception enjoyed for its own sake (or even undertaken for its own sake, since negative esthetic experiences are still in a sense esthetic). It thus applies to the direct enjoyment of the colors of a painting, or of the sheer sound of an orchestra, regardless of how or whether they contribute to any hypothetical unity. Again, at the first level of organization, it applies to the appreciation of the details of the picture or of the motifs of a symphony, without necessary reference to the role of these in the total composition. At a somewhat higher level, it applies to a sense of the connections between contiguous details or motifs in point-to-point or moment-to-moment relationship.

The mode by which we directly perceive the sensuous medium, its primitive elements, and their closest interrelationships, is the one I wish to contrast with that of synoptic comprehension. I shall call it the mode of *immediate apprehension*. It is, I believe, what Whitehead had in mind when he wrote, "The habit of art is the habit of enjoying vivid values."[2] Further on, in a discussion of esthetic appreciation in non-artistic realms, he exhibits his awareness of both modes: "A factory . . . is an organism exhibiting a variety of vivid values. What we want to train is the habit of apprehending such an organism in its completeness."[3] In part, the contrast between the two is that between experience and contemplation. Immediate apprehension is our response to a direct contact—our recognition of Whitehead's "vivid values." Synoptic comprehension is to some extent conceptual: it is our realization of the form of what we have perceived—Whitehead's "organism". (The same

[1] Leo Stein, *op. cit.*, p. 46.
[2] Alfred North Whitehead, *Science and the Modern World,* New York: The Macmillan Company, 1935, p. 287.
[3] *Ibid.*, pp. 287–88.

contrast could be made with respect to the stages of artistic creation, as Wordsworth suggested in his famous definition of poetry.)

Of the two modes, it is the immediate that enjoys both temporal and logical priority in our perception of art. Temporal, in the sense that our appreciation of an esthetic object usually begins with our apprehension of its sensuous qualities and, especially in the case of a time-art, of its details; logical, because, in my view, enjoyment of such apprehension can lead to some measure of esthetic satisfaction whether or not it is accompanied by synoptic comprehension, and whether or not such comprehension, if achieved, finds a worthy object. On the other hand, one can, to be sure, regard pure structure esthetically, i.e. contemplate it for its own sake. But if its embodiment, from the point of view of immediate apprehension, is negative (as, for instance, a malignant tumor or its picture would be to most people), one is unlikely to derive esthetic pleasure from the structure, no matter how perfect it may be. When the embodiment is neutral, as in pure geometry, the esthetic appeal of the structure can indeed reveal itself to synoptic comprehension; but the neutrality reveals one important distinction between mathematics and art. Mathematics, unlike art, fails to respond to immediate apprehension.

The synoptic mode, for its part, is essential to the perception of esthetic objects as *objects*, and particularly of works of art as individual *works*. To this extent I agree with Stein: to see the object as an object is to perceive its unity, that is, to understand its structure. But the achievement of this kind of comprehension is far from necessary to the appreciation of esthetic quality; indeed, as I shall try to show, some kinds of art seem to resist it.

I should like to approach this point through a short discussion of what is often called "natural beauty"; but since I do not wish to introduce a phrase so full of literary connotations and implying so many unanswerable questions,[4] I shall try to avoid them by using the somewhat cumbersome term "the natural esthetic continuum" to mean the natural world, existing in space and time, as esthetically perceived. Whatever the structure of the continuum may be, no human mind is capable of conceiving, much less perceiving it —except possibly through the rare gift of mystical insight. What the ordinary mind experiences is never the (space-time) continuum as a whole, but what one might call a spatio-temporal cross-section, bound together by point-to-point, moment-to-moment, area-to-area relationships. There is no guarantee that these relationships will produce a perceptible unity; the chances are that they will not. We cannot, therefore, be sure that our cross-section can be comprehended as an esthetic object—but we can still enjoy its immediacy. Let us call such a cross-section an *esthetic surface.*

One can think of many kinds of surfaces: a starry night, a mountain landscape, a bird in flight, a flower. Some of them—e.g. the starry night—would resist attempts to force them into some kind of esthetic structure. They stubbornly remain sections of the apparently amorphous continuum, permitting only immediate apprehension. Others—e.g. the flower—are readily grasped as formal unities and hence are easily turned by the observer into esthetic objects. Most— e.g. the landscape, the bird—are borderline cases. On the one hand, their immediate appeal as surface is usually undeniable. On the other, even though it takes real effort to impose form on a landscape, that is just what the artistically trained eye often tries to do. And for many observers, much of the fascination of watching the living bird comes not just from the immediate apprehension of its sensuous qualities

[4] For an interesting discussion of some of these, see R. W. Hepburn's essay *Contemporary Aesthetics and the Neglect of Natural Beauty,* in Bernard Williams and Alan Montefiore, eds., *British Analytical Philosophy,* London: Routledge and Kegan Paul, 1966, pp. 285–310.

but also from a realization of its specialized anatomy, of its apparently complex pattern of instincts, and of its role in the total ecology—in a word, of its structure. (Some of this interest even adheres to photographs of wild creatures, to habitat groups in museums, and to recordings of bird song.)

The natural surface pushes, then, in two directions— toward the continuum and toward the object—although it usually disappoints our efforts at complete synoptic comprehension. This, I think, is one reason why the bird-lover, once granted a view of, say, a scarlet tanager, finds it very hard to stop looking at it. It would be like leaving a theater before the play is over—only this play is never over, because it has no beginning and no ending. A real play satisfies us through the completion of its form. The play of nature tantalizes us through its constant hints of a never fully realized form. It is just here that we find a counterbalance for the preceding argument in favor of the priority of immediate apprehension. For its delights are ultimately insufficient in themselves; they need the complement of structural comprehension. (For the same reason the bird lover hates to stop listening to a long-continued bird song. The nightingale often offers this kind of song at night, when, because of the surrounding quiet, it is bound to catch the attention. It is no wonder that, under these circumstances, the apparent endlessness of the outpouring has given rise to the myths of "Eternal passion! Eternal pain!")

There is another reason why the bird lover extracts every possible moment from his tanager, and this brings us to the contrast between natural esthetic products (to use a neutral term that can denote both surfaces and objects) and those that are man-made: once gone, the former are very likely unrecapturable; the latter are, in principle, repeatable. The tanager may never return, every flower is fading even as we look at it, the effect of a landscape is dependent on transitory weather conditions; but one can presumably return to a picture or to a piece of music as often as one likes (for "it *endures*"). From this point of view, there is a borderline case between natural and man-made objects: the rock, the piece of driftwood, created by nature but transformed by virtue of its position on a mantelpiece into —perhaps not a work of art, but at least something that approaches an artistic object.

"Artistic," as I use the word, refers to esthetic products that are man-made—but it is not equivalent to "esthetic, man-made". In my view a slag-heap (certainly man-made) could possibly have esthetic value, but it would still not be artistic. Its value, whether considered as accidentally produced, or as adduced by the sensitive eye of some beholder, is analogous to that of a natural scene. Artistic quality, I fear, can only be determined by invoking the intentional fallacy (which I consider no fallacy—unless it is the fallacy of believing that there is an intentional fallacy). Artistic quality is *intentionally produced* esthetic quality, whether in articles normally classified as useful or in what are usually called works of art.

I do not wish to push the distinction between artistic objects and works of art, although I believe that it can be a useful one. If we accept the definition of an artistic object as any intentionally produced esthetic object, then the term can be applied to chairs and bedspreads and lampshades as well as to the members of the more restricted category of *bona fide* works of art. But since the line delimiting the smaller class is very fuzzy (when, for example, does a building become a work of art?), I prefer not to try to draw it. I wish rather to examine a far more important distinction: that between artistic surfaces on the one hand and artistic objects (including works of art) on the other. For not all artistic products are objects. Some, which defeat attempt at synoptic comprehension and respond to the immediate mode of perception only, must accordingly be classified as artistic surfaces.

We must now return to an argument of the first essay and look at it from a slightly different point of view. What I there called the internal environment of representational works of art we can now see as imaginative re-creations of the natural esthetic continuum. A picture, for example, is embedded in a visual, spatial continuum. In the case of a literary work, the continuum is the entire world of thought and action. I think we can generalize to the extent of asserting that all examples of representational art can be perceived as cross-sections of an imaginary continuum, and hence as artistic surfaces. In order to qualify further as artistic objects, they must reward synoptic comprehension as well—but certainly not all of them do. There are so-called "works of art" that exhibit, in detail, skill of execution, sensuous beauty, profundity of ideas—whatever critical norm you may wish to adduce; but, lacking a controlling formal structure, they are not, in the final sense, artistic objects, and hence *not* works of art. I am not trying to contrast here "closed" with "open" form: open form, even though it may be hard to grasp, is still form. I am contrasting those products that are sufficiently formed to reveal a unified structure with those that are not.

Many examples of Renaissance and Baroque decoration (like the Pozzo ceiling already mentioned) fail to qualify as works of art. This does not prevent one from deriving keen enjoyment from their immediate apprehension as surface (even when, unlike the Pozzo ceiling, they cannot be recognized as participating in a larger formal unity).

Less happy examples are afforded by numerous storytelling pictures, especially of the nineteenth century. Here the environment is as much temporal as spatial, for the representation is a cross-section of a narrative as well as of a visual scene. Our attempts to impose a narrative structure—to re-create the "before" and "after" phases of the depicted moment—often prevent us from enjoying what purely visual values the picture may have, minimal as they may be. (It has been only recently that our training in viewing abstractions has taught us to concentrate on the immediacy of the depicted detail in some of the pre-Raphaelite pictures and to disregard their deficiency in over-all structure and their frequent sentimentality of subject-matter.)

Non-objective painting, too, can suggest a continuum, albeit an artificial one. Those canvases of the action school that are filled with visual events—and those that seem peculiarly empty of them—alike suggest that the kind of thing we see within the frame is also going on beyond its boundaries, and that the edge delimits a cross-section of an indefinitely extending continuum. Many of these works, including some of the most celebrated, seem to be apprehensible only in this way. Thus some of Jackson Pollock's late paintings seem to be surfaces rather than works of art. One rationale offered for action painting—the plea that each work should be taken as the expression of an action of the artist rather than as a pure object—only confirms this judgment.

I shall not discuss architecture in this connection, except to note that its internal and external environments are the same; in other words, probably alone among the major arts, it exists directly within the natural continuum. Music, by contrast, as I have already pointed out, is unique among the arts in lacking in principle any embedding continuum. But just as some abstract sculpture can appear so hermetic as, exceptionally, to defy one to supply any surrounding internal environment, so some music (to which we might also apply the word "abstract" in a special sense) runs counter to the rule and seems not only to suggest but even to depend on an artificial continuum. I have suggested that "totally determined" serial music gives the effect of being a segment of an indefinitely extensible twelve-tone continuum. Similarly, "non-determined" music, whether the sequence of events is left up to the performer or to pure chance, may imply a continuum that often seems to combine the purely musical with the quasi-dramatic. The two determinisms of formula and fortune lead to the same result: the arbitrary way in which such products begin and end and the fortuitous nature of their inner connections ensure that they can at best be experienced only as surfaces.

From the foregoing one might conclude that whenever music seems to suggest or demand that it be heard as a segment of an artificial continuum, it will by virtue of that characteristic resist synoptic comprehension. I believe this to be true, although I cannot demonstrate it. The converse is of course false; for there is a great deal of music that, while resting comfortably within its extremes and making no demands on a hypothetical environment, nevertheless cannot be structurally comprehended. I suspect that Wagner's music-dramas and some of Strauss's longer tone-poems fall into this category. It is certainly true that what many of us are enjoying (if that is the right word) through long stretches of, say, *Also sprach Zarathustra* or *Siegfried* is surface. Even if one could combine Schenker and Lorenz, and prove that each Wagnerian act could be analyzed as a structural unity that organically incorporated every smallest detail, that would not prove that each act could be so *heard*. Synoptic comprehension is indeed partly conceptual —but only partly so. It is still a mode of perception. There is probably a limit in sheer time to what the human ear can take in structurally; when this limit is overstepped, the listener falls back on immediate apprehension. (Or else he turns gratefully to the discrete operatic forms of Mozart.)

The compositions that are ultimately the most satisfying —the only ones that, according to my usage, deserve the name of composition—are those that invite and reward both modes of perception. I have already said that the immediate mode usually precedes the synoptic in one's approach to any work of art; in the case of music, which can be comprehended structurally only after it has been experienced in time, this is necessarily so. This does not mean, however, that immediate apprehension is merely a phase of perception that one has to get through in order to enjoy the true bliss of understanding structure. (That applies to mathematics—not to music.) The ideal hearing of a composition is one that enjoys both modes simultaneously, that savors each detail all the more for realizing its role in the form of the whole. (It is this kind of hearing that makes possible the renewed enjoyment of suspense in familiar works that I have discussed in the second essay.)

Most practical instruction in performance is directed toward the encouragement of immediate apprehension. Beauty of tone, careful phrasing, instrumental balance, rhythmic articulation—these are usually presented as means of projecting a series of pleasing sounds or interesting passages toward an audience that is presumably incapable of synoptic comprehension anyway. As a counterbalance to this approach, the foregoing essays have been devoted primarily to what might be called the performance of form. But it is equally true that modern music theory tends to stress the unifying aspects of form to the extent that it seems to accept as valid only the mode of perception that "best appeases our lust for inventing structures." [5] I readily admit to such a lust, but I must also confess an equally unholy delight in what Edmund Gurney calls "the successive notes and smallest fragments, as they turn up moment after moment, throughout any piece of music which is keenly and characteristically enjoyed." [6] Gurney, indeed, represents a polar extreme to the formalistic views in vogue today, for his claim as to the primacy of the detail is complete: ". . . however organic the whole result may appear when fully known, the parts may here be said, in the truest sense, to be more important and primary than the whole; for the whole being a combination of parts successively (and many of them to a great extent independently) enjoyed, can only be impressive so far as the parts are impressive; and the impressiveness can only be perceived by

[5] J. K. Randall, *A Report from Princeton*, in *Perspectives of New Music*, III/2 (Spring-Summer 1965), 85.

[6] Edmund Gurney, *The Power of Sound*, New York: Basic Books, 1966 (reprint of London, 1880 edn.), p. 214.

focussing the attention on each of the parts in turn, and cannot be summed up in rapid comprehensive glances." [7] Few of us will follow Gurney that far; yet the example of his healthily hedonistic attention to the musical surface should stand as a constant reminder that there are alternatives to the rapt admiration of bloodless formulas and jejune diagrams to which our lust for structures sometimes leads us today.

[7] *Ibid.*, p. 97.

# INDEX

# Index of Names and Works